PARAMETERS OF
BRITISH NAVAL POWER
1650–1850

EXETER MARITIME STUDIES
General Editor: Stephen Fisher

EXETER MARITIME STUDIES · NUMBER SEVEN

PARAMETERS OF BRITISH NAVAL POWER 1650–1850

Edited by

MICHAEL DUFFY

UNIVERSITY
of
EXETER
PRESS

First Published in 1992 by
University of Exeter Press
Reed Hall
Streatham Drive
Exeter EX4 4QR
UK

British Library Cataloguing in Publication Data

A catalogue record of this book is available from the British Library

ISBN 0 85989 385 5

Typeset in New Century Schoolbook by Nigel Code

Printed in the Great Britain by Antony Rowe Ltd., Chippenham

Contents

Acknowledgements

The editor of this collection wishes to express his gratitude above all to Nigel Code for his patience, understanding and craftsmanship in the production of this volume; to the contributors, particularly Jeremy Black and Nicholas Rodger, for their unfailing helpfulness in its preparation; and to Roger Knight and Dan Baugh for reading the typescript and offering helpful advice.

1

INTRODUCTION

Michael Duffy

This volume has collected together papers relating to a common theme presented by David Davies, Jeremy Black and Roger Morriss at Dartington maritime history conferences organised by the Centre for Maritime Historical Studies of Exeter University (chapters II, III and VII), together with Nicholas Rodger's 1991 Harte Lecture at Exeter University (chapter V), Michael Duffy's 1990 Autumn Lecture to the Society for Nautical Research (chapter IV), and a further article by Jeremy Black stemming from work associated with his recent *War for America. The Fight for Independence 1775–1783* (chapter VI).

In recent years there has developed a more questioning approach to the traditional triumphalist version of British naval history.[1] Now that Britain has lost its naval supremacy it is possible to be more objective about the grounds on which that former supremacy was based. No longer is it taken for granted that Britannia was pre-ordained to rule the waves, nor that ruling the waves gave automatic hegemony either over Europe or the world. The advantages that Britain achieved were never constant and had to be continually worked for in ever fluctuating situations. The articles in this volume continue this questioning by showing the tortuous path by which Britain groped and struggled towards gaining and endeavouring to maintain naval supremacy, by examining the obstacles along that path, and by considering just what that supremacy could in practice achieve.

David Davies shows that the creation of a great battlefleet was merely the start of the problem, only raising the next issue of what to do with it. Both he and Jeremy Black, in his two articles, show that its mobilisation in peacetime could have important diplomatic effects in the right circumstances, though this game of bluff could also spectacularly miscarry if the government mistook its appreciation of the respective balance of forces, as the Younger Pitt found out to his cost in 1791.

Mobilisation would however be less effective without a clear strategic plan of how to use this naval power if the bluff was called, and David Davies shows how the later Stuarts struggled to arrive at a strategic plan first to confront the Dutch and then the French. He makes the important point of how seventeenth-century values of honour and reputation, significant for both Republic and Monarchy, and their naval commanders, alike, could threaten to disrupt rational planning, particularly over the issue of the salute to the flag which was involved in the English claim to the sovereignty of the seas. The Dutch Wars provided the planners with their best ever opportunity to embark on a so-called 'Blue Water' strategy, devoid of heavy military commitment to a continental war,[2] but David Davies provides a timely caution against regarding 'Blue Water' as any clear-cut strategic solution. It was not a single simple option, and its implementation failed of effect because the planners were constantly torn between the various possible 'Blue Water' ways forward—either a concentrated attack on the Dutch battlefleet, or an assault on Dutch commerce, or amphibious landings on the Dutch coast.

David Davies also argues persuasively that Charles II and his brother James were concerned at the threat from the rapidly expanding French naval power and that they planned thoroughly and seriously the strategic deployment of the navy in the event of a French war. It was this plan which formed the basis of the arrangements made by the new Williamite regime when that war finally came in 1689, though this rapidly revealed logistical obstacles to its operation which are discussed in Michael Duffy's article.

Jeremy Black's first contribution to the volume emphasises a major constraint on the free use of Britain's naval power by its strategic directors: the fact that Britain lacked a large army, which tied the navy down as substitute for the many roles that military power should otherwise have performed. Principal among these was defence against invasion. While it is often maintained that France lacked the means to land a large army in Britain, the events of 1688 showed what could be done, and finished quickly, by an invading army as small as 15,000 with internal support. Until after the defeat of the French invasion attempt of 1759, no British government was altogether sure how much internal Jacobite support would rally to a French or Spanish landing in such force, nor at the end of the eighteenth-century could anyone be sure of the Irish reaction if such a force landed there. 1688, and also 1796, showed moreover that in particular weather conditions even the navy could not be a certain protection against such landings. These episodes however only served to highlight the importance of the navy to national defence. The threat of invasion therefore was an important means by

2

which France in particular could deprive Britain of the strategic initiative, since it imposed a degree of paralysis on British operations until a substantial naval defence was established, and thereafter tied down powerful British squadrons guarding against an attack that might never come.

The lack of a large army also required the navy to substitute for it in other ways: to provide some of the co-operation in military operations on the continent expected by Britain's European allies, particularly in the Mediterranean; and to provide manpower, artillery and haulage on land, as well as transportation by sea, in support of the army's overseas colonial expeditions.[3] Each of these absorbed resources that could not then be deployed to advantage in the purely maritime struggle – the defeat of the enemy's battlefleet, the defence of British trade,[4] and the destruction of enemy maritime commerce. This plethora of responsibilities placed upon the navy left it frequently very hard pressed, no matter how large was its actual numerical superiority over the navies of its opponents (and at times this was small or non-existant). Rarely did it have the ability to do all that was demanded of it. In 1757, at a time when the British fleet was nearly double that of France, the Secretary of State for the North, Lord Holdernesse, turned down a request from Britain's Prussian ally, Frederick the Great, for naval support in the Baltic, explaining that:

...I am sorry to tell you, that the strength of the English marine is not equal perhaps to what is thought abroad, owing to great want of sailors; and yet His Majesty must have a squadron in the Mediterranean, equal at least to the Toulon fleet; one in the Channel, to keep the squadrons of Brest and Rochfort in respect; one in North America; a considerable one in the West Indies, which from the nature of the trade winds is necessarily divided, and one in the East Indies.[5]

The expectation of the later Stuarts was that a French war would assume the same shape as the Dutch, with hard fought, concentrated battlefleet actions. When after 1692 however, the French switched their policy away from fleet actions to commerce raiding, while keeping their fleet available as a potential threat, English strategy too had to change, leading to changes in the composition of the fleet with the need for more smaller cruising ships for commerce protection, and to the dispersal of the fleet to meet the many responsibilities outlined above. One policy that the Royal Navy developed far ahead of its French rival was the establishment of naval bases overseas: at Minorca in 1709, English Harbour, Antigua, and Port Royal, Jamaica, in the 1730s, and Halifax, Nova Scotia, between 1757 and 1759. Careening, naval stores supply, victualling and hospital facilities were established at these bases, thus enabling the Navy to maintain an all-year-round presence in permanent stations as opposed to the French practise of sending out squadrons from Europe for short periods each year. Two naval yards in the Caribbean, where France had none, enabled Britain to establish local superiority for most of the mid-eighteenth-century wars, while the establishment of a permanent naval presence at Halifax in 1757 was a vital part of the throttling of the supply line to French Canada which led to its final surrender in 1760.[6]

Overseas support bases thus extended considerably the parameters of British naval power, albeit at great expense in ships, men and money, which tied down resources, limited alternative strategic deployments, and exposed the small squadrons on these stations to the risk of being overwhelmed by any larger force sent out from France. The French by contrast chose to concentrate rather than scatter their naval resources. British policy was torn between the conflicting demands of the need to disperse its navy to exercise command of the seas, protecting British trade and destroying French trade and colonial resources, and the need to maintain that command by being able to concentrate sufficient force to defeat any challenge to it mounted from France. Only in the middle of the eighteenth century did a strategy emerge which rationalised this widespread deployment to make the most economical use of the resources available. The new strategy was that of maintaining a powerful 'Western Squadron' in the Bay of Biscay and the Channel Approaches, which could guard against invasion of the British Isles, protect incoming and outgoing British trade and intercept that of the French, and prevent the French from sending forces overseas to defend their colonies from attack or to attack those of Britain, all at the same time.

David Davies shows that some of the advantages of such a strategy were seen as early as in the 1668 instructions for Sir Thomas Allin's squadron. The problems in the way of setting it up however were enormous, and they are detailed, together with their eventual laborious resolution, in Michael Duffy's article. Primarily it was achieved by expanding operational capabilities through developing an entirely new support system from a new domestic naval base begun in 1690 at Plymouth, and in general it would seem that British naval administrators were much more impressed with the need for an adequate supporting infrastructure to maintain their ships at sea than were their rivals. This was indeed a matter of both sheer necessity and better finance. With Britain, its empire and its trade so vulnerable to maritime attack, there was felt to be an urgent need to keep the ships of the Royal Navy at sea for as long as possible. The resultant wear and tear, however, created far more maintenance demands which had to be met as far as facilities allowed if British naval power was to survive. A major factor extending the parameters of British naval power was, therefore, the dry-dock capacity of British dockyards which facilitated the major overhaul of warships, and with twenty-three dry docks in 1793-6 as against eight in French and eight in Spanish yards, the Royal Navy could turn round more ships at a faster rate than its rivals.[7] This was a capacity of which the Western Squadron had particular need, seeking to operate as it did in the area most exposed to the elements of all those that the Navy endeavoured to hold.

Michael Duffy shows how the Western Squadron system was developed by trial and error, though its evolution was accelerated by the mid-eighteenth-century threat of invasion and, as he and Jeremy Black indicate, by the particular needs of the later stages of the War of the Austrian Succession to defend British colonial successes in order to use them at the negotiating table so as to counterbalance French military success in the Low Countries. That the policy should be so spectacularly successful in the middle of the eighteenth century, however, was the result of two developments which deserve greater recognition. The first of these was the rapid growth of the French empire and its wealth in the first half of the eighteenth century. French colonial trade grew in value from an average 35.2 million livres per annum in 1715-20 to 137.9 millions in 1749-55. The size and value of French overseas commerce continued to expand until 1790: its share of world trade grew from 8 per cent in 1720 to 12 per cent in 1780, and its merchant fleet from 150,000 tons in 1730 to 574,000 in 1785.[8] It now had far more to lose in a maritime war than in the wars between 1689-1713, and its government finances, and hence its ability to wage war, were more dependent on its colonial commerce. This obliged the French to send out their navy to defend that trade and empire, which exposed it to defeat as in 1747, and it enabled Britain to fight effectively on its strengths at sea and overseas rather than on France's strength on the Continent – provided Britain could shut off France's ability to despatch that strength overseas. In 1759 this task was triumphantly achieved by the Western Squadron, which simultaneously defended Britain from invasion and protected British attacks on the French empire in Canada and the West Indies against interruption from France.

The second of the new developments enabling the success of the Western Squadron strategy is described by Jeremy Black in his first and at the end of his second contributions to this volume, where he points to the effect of the altered diplomatic situation. He convincingly stresses the importance of diplomacy in freeing the navy from some of its overload of commitments. Thus between 1716 and 1731, it was the French alliance with Britain that released the navy from home defence and

5

enabled it to send powerful squadrons to the Baltic, the Mediterranean and the West Indies. The collapse of that alliance in the later year reawakened fear of invasion, forced the retention of much of the navy in home waters, and created a state of almost perpetual crisis until the invasion threat was at last smashed by Boscawen and Hawke in 1759. However it may have been equally important to Britain's eventual success that two treaties were made by Britain's ally of the 1740s, Austria, with Britain's enemies of the 1740s, Spain (in 1752) and France (in 1756), which paradoxically actually considerably strengthened the British position in the later stages of that crisis. Spain was thereby encouraged into a position of neutrality from which it did not emerge until 1762. This enabled the British navy to concentrate on and to achieve the destruction of the French navy before the intervention of the Spanish fleet, which would have otherwise brought the numerical balance of opposing naval forces into near parity and made the British task immeasurably more difficult. Nor did the advantages to Britain end there, for the Austrian understanding with Spain and France neutralised Italy and released the navy from its obligations in former wars of providing direct assistance to military operations on the shores of the Mediterranean. Lastly, Austria's alliance with France in 1756, which at the time was widely regarded as a diplomatic defeat for Britain, turned into an unrecognised asset when coupled to Austrian neutrality in the French conflict with Britain, for it removed the French threat to the Austrian Netherlands and to Holland beyond them, again releasing the navy from defensive commitments. More naval resources were thus released to concentrate on the purely maritime aspects of the war with France. Following the lead provocatively given by Daniel Baugh, who has asserted that Britain's lack of continental commitments enabled it to outlast France, Spain and Holland in the War of American Independence,[9] Black argues that the Franco-Austrian alliance of 1756 in fact stabilised the political situation in western Europe until the early 1790s, hence enabling Britain to limit the extent of its continental commitments, and that among the main beneficiaries of this was the Royal Navy.

Even in this considerably improved situation however, naval resources were still extremely stretched. Although naval administrators were perpetually worried about warship building, the number of ships available was not in fact the greatest problem. The Navy expanded from 173 ships (100,000 tons) in 1688 to 755 ships (over 500,000 tons) in sea service in 1809. Britain's vast merchant marine (its tonnage double France's, four times Holland's and over ten times Spain's in 1785) was sustained by by far the biggest private shipbuilding capacity in Europe, to which the Royal Navy increasingly turned from the middle of the eighteenth century for its needs. From 29 percent of ships of the line in 1688–1755, the private yards built 52 percent between 1756–1815, freeing the naval dockyards to concentrate more on the operational maintenance of the fleet. This was a resource which the French were acutely conscious that they lacked.[10]

The greatest problem, as Holdernesse's letter quoted above indicates, was shortage of manpower to meet all the tasks that the navy was being called upon to perform, and manpower constraints indeed constituted a further parameter to British naval power. Jeremy Black has shown the impact of manpower shortages in impeding mobilisation and restricting the impact of either British diplomacy or war effort on specific occasions, both in his contributions here (looking at 1757 and 1778) and elsewhere.[11] The problem was still present in 1793, when the Home Secretary and war minister, Henry Dundas, echoed Holdernesse in replying to a request from the army chief of staff in Flanders for seamen to participate in the siege of Dunkirk. He had already sent a large squadron to the West Indies in March and a fleet of 22 of the line to the Mediterranean in April-May, and now he declared that he was unable to send out a fleet to the Channel equal to the exertions the French were making, while another fleet had to be ready for the West Indies in a few weeks, and at least five ships had to be despatched to the East Indies in the autumn, so that it was impossible to spare seamen for operations out of their element. He added that: 'Against another year I suppose we may have any number of Ships at Sea that we can wish, but in the first year of a War, this Country must always arm slowly, because its Trade must not be annihilated.'[12]

Dundas was right to point to the difficulty of tapping Britain's 118,000 merchant seamen, in order to expand the Navy from its 1792 peacetime level (17,000) to the level it needed to fulfil its wartime demands, without crippling the mercantile activities that provided the financial sinews for the war effort. He was however wildly optimistic in believing that this was simply a mobilisation problem, for the tasks and manpower needs of the Navy were escalating war by war, from a peak of 44,861 in 1748, to 84,797 in 1762, 107,446 in 1783, and to a high over all former times of 142,098 men borne in 1810.[13]

The nature of the manpower problem is considered in this volume by Nicholas Rodger and also in part by Roger Morriss. Nicholas Rodger analyses the heart of the problem down to a basic shortage of men with particular vital skills, which took at least two years of sea-going experience to acquire. He points out that this elite group of petty officers and able seamen who could work the sails aloft constituted only a fifth of a ship of the line's company, but without them the ship could not be sailed. This important point serves to highlight an often unappreciated factor behind British success in its two most successful naval wars of this period, the Seven Years' War and the Napoleonic War, in that by catching so much French shipping at sea by an unexpected attack before the declaration of war (1755–6) or by a surprise declaration of war (1803), the Royal Navy was able to inflict an initial crippling blow on its French counterpart by capturing large numbers of these skilled and indispensable French petty officers and able seamen. By May 1757 over 14,406 French seamen lay in British prisons, including 4,703 petty officers and ables - sufficient to work up to thirty ships of the line.[14]

While it did its utmost to deprive its opponents of this necessary commodity, Nicholas Rodger shows how the mid-eighteenth-century Royal Navy sought to secure it for itself by the personal relationship established between captains, responsible for recruiting their own crews, and seamen who knew and trusted them. Recent research, in which Nicholas Rodger has been prominent, has re-evaluated the qualitative differences between service in the Navy and in the merchant marine, and has overthrown previous assumptions by showing a balance of advantages by no means unfavourable to the Navy.[15] Here he shows how, in these circumstances, personal relationships which encouraged volunteering could play an important part in naval recruitment, either by professional acquaintance to secure the ables, or by local connection to secure the landsmen and ordinary seamen necessary to haul on ropes and man the guns. The Admiralty's replacement of this personal recruitment system by increasing use of the Impress Service in the later eighteenth-century broke that bond and heightened problems of recruitment, retention and relations on board ship.

Throughout the period under consideration in this volume, contemporary criticism was directed at the use of the press. Nevertheless it survived into the nineteenth century, and indeed increased in use as a recruiting tool as volunteering failed to keep pace with the Navy's ever expanding needs, because, as Roger Morriss indicates, no other acceptable method could be found to man the fleet in a hurry. When the Victorians felt it politically unacceptable to press the naval manpower needed for the Crimean war and sought to recruit solely by bounties instead, the result was nearly disastrous.[16] The country was not prepared to accept the bureaucratic interference and regulation necessary to register all seamen on the French system (which was in any case less praised in France than by British reformers[17]) nor the cost of maintaining either a larger peacetime naval establishment or a paid reserve beyond the officer corps. Yet even the press could only raise a limited number of men in a hurry. With so much of British merchant shipping and seamen scattered throughout the world, extensive forced recruitment was dependent on the seasonal return of the trade in the latter part of each year. Roger Morriss supports Admiral Cockburn's contention that the country got the naval manpower (and the manpower problems) that it was prepared to pay for.

The issue however was not just one of recruitment but also of retention, for the Navy lost manpower by desertion and sickness. Desertion was endemic in the wartime navy: probably some 40,000 of the 185,000 enlistments in the Seven Years' War, 42,000 altogether in the War of American Independence and again in the French Revolutionary War.[18] It was a drain, but its impact can be exaggerated: as Nicholas Rodger has shown, the desertion rate in the Seven Years' War was contained at a replacable seven percent per annum.[19] Roger Morriss defends the pragmatism of Cockburn on this issue also: higher pay would always be bettered by the merchant marine, so that better treatment in the Navy, greater attention and care by officers for their crews, was the necessary remedy. The other major aspect of the manpower retention problem was sickness, and this is considered by Michael Duffy in relation to the Western Squadron. The capacity of sickness to devastate crews, to the extent that they might no longer be able to work their ships safely, was a problem that beset all navies. The crowded, badly-ventilated, constantly damp living conditions on warships were virulent breeding grounds of disease among men weakened by constant hard labour and poor nutrition. Perhaps because they were the most dependent for national survival on keeping their ships at sea, the British seem to have made greater efforts than their maritime rivals at coming to grips with this problem, particularly in the second half of the eighteenth century. They certainly felt that they were more attentive to ship hygeine, nutrition and hospital care than their French counterparts, and, indeed, on the two occasions when the French established control of home waters, in 1690 and 1779, it was the violent impact of disease which drove them back to port rather than the efforts of the Royal Navy. Typhus and above all scurvy were the main scourges. The former was containable through better hygeine and nutrition, the latter through regular revictualling with fresh meat and vegetables. However the regularity of supply had to be painstakingly and expensively constructed, and it was always precarious. When in the American War it broke down, of 175,993 men raised between 1776 and 1780, 18,545 died of disease, compared to 1,243 killed in action.[20]

The American War increased the demands made upon the navy by tying it down to the support of the army in continental war, this time on the American continent. It had never been comfortable in trying to fulfil this role in Europe, and Jeremy Black's second contribution to this volume shows that it fared no better in America. Perhaps it might have achieved more had it been larger and equipped with the right ships, but

Lord North's attempts to maintain political unity at home by keeping costs down to what he felt would be an acceptable level proved to be a false economy, both in impeding the navy's performance in the purely American stage of the war, and also by delaying for too long the far more extensive mobilisation required when France prepared to intervene in the struggle—which resulted in it having to contest the early years of the conflict with France and Spain at a disadvantage.[21]

This is probably as good an illustration as could be found of another major parameter of British naval power—financial constraint. Many recent studies of the French navy have shown how this was an all-pervasive limitation on French naval power,[22] and generally in wartime British governments and public alike were far more ready to direct resources into their navy than their French counterpart.[23] However, a navy was an expensive instrument, and in peacetime there was an irresistible temptation for harassed ministers, looking to cut the burden of unpopular taxes, to cut naval expenditure to the bone. The Pelham ministry in the early 1750s and the Grenville ministry between 1763 and 1765, provide ready examples of this which set back naval efficiency considerably. The shock of the loss of America ensured that this example would not be followed after 1783, and Jeremy Black shows how the Pitt government's willingness to invest in the rebuilding of the fleet enabled him to use its rapid mobilisation to capitalise on France's inability to make a similar extra financial effort, and so to achieve major diplomatic successes in 1787 and 1790. Equally indicative of the financial parameters of naval power, he withdrew from confrontation with Russia in the 1791 when he saw that parliament was unwilling to finance the necessary naval armament.

The total defeat of Napoleonic France in 1814-15 however, led successive post-war governments to ignore naval advice in order to reap the resultant peace dividend. The national horror at the immense load of taxes that had been necessary to finance victory over Napoleon lasted to the middle of the nineteenth century, so that yet again the Navy was stretched to the limits both to fulfill the demands made upon it to support the immediate needs of British diplomacy and to maintain and develope the fleet and its infrastructure for any future major war. In 1833, with a squadron deployed blockading the Dutch coast and another at Lisbon protecting Portugal, the Navy had no ships to spare to answer Turkish pleas for assistance against Egyptian attack, and, since neither Cabinet nor Parliament was willing to pay to man and equip more ships, Russia was able to step in and do what Britain failed to do, acquiring a dominant influence over Turkey in the process. The Foreign Secretary, Lord Palmerston, redeemed the situation in 1840 but only by means of a colossal bluff in which the Navy (with auxiliary help from Russian,

10

Austrian and Turkish ships) forced the Egyptian army out of Syria in the face of a superior, hostile, French Mediteranean fleet.[24]

In the last contribution to this volume, Roger Morriss shows that it was this financial constraint, rather than any rooted aversion to new technology, that held back the Navy's exploration and adoption of steam power. His re-examination of the person frequently cited as the archetype reactionary naval officer and administrator of the period, Sir George Cockburn, shows a man conscious of the practical needs of maintaining seapower and struggling to meet them within a limited budget, yet willing to experiment when the funds and the right technology appeared to be available. Roger Morriss sees Cockburn rather as exemplifying the solid professionalism which had been at the heart of British naval administration (far more than at that of the French[25]), and which enabled the Navy to survive financial constraints, to tackle pragmatically and to overcome the many strategic, technological and logistical problems which it encountered on the way to establishing naval supremacy.

May 1992

NOTES

1. Paul Kennedy was among the early leaders in *The Rise and Fall of British Naval Mastery* (London, 1976), by showing how dependent was British mastery on economic circumstances. Edward Ingram was prepared to be far more iconoclastic by challenging the achievement of the British naval super-hero, Nelson ('Illusions of Victory: The Nile, Copenhagen, and Trafalgar Revisited,' Military Affairs, 48 [1984], No.3, 140–3). A well-balanced critique is provided by the articles in J. Black and P. Woodfine, eds, *The British Navy and the Use of Naval Power in the Eighteenth Century* (Leicester, 1988).
2. See D.A. Baugh, 'Great Britain's "Blue Water" Policy, 1689–1815,' *International History Review*, 10 (1988), 33–58.
3. For examples of the latter see D. Syrett, ed., *The Siege and Capture of Havana: 1762* (N[avy] R[ecords] S[ociety], vol. 114, 1970); M. Duffy, *Soldiers, Sugar and Seapower. The British Expeditions to the West Indies and the War against Revolutionary France* (Oxford, 1987); and for the disastrous repercussions when the Navy refused to perform this role see R. Harding, *Amphibious Warfare in the Eighteenth Century. The British Expedition to the West Indies, 1740–1742* (Woodbridge, 1991).
4. This vital but often overlooked activity was arguably the most important naval contribution to British success, for it secured the financial sinews that were the particular strength of the British war effort. See A. Pearsall, 'The Royal Navy and the Protection of Trade in the Eighteenth Century' in *Guerres et Paix 1660–1815. Journées franco-anglaises*

d'histoire de la Marine, Vol.1 (Vincennes, 1987), 149–62; R.P. Crowhurst, *The Defence of British Trade 1689–1815* (London, 1977) and 'The Admiralty and the Convoy System in the Seven Years War', *The Mariner's Mirror*, 57 (1971), 163–73; and D. Syrett, 'The Organisation of British Trade Convoys during the American War 1775–83', *Mariner's Mirror*, 62 (1976), 169-81.

5. Holdernesse to Mitchell, 5 July 1757, quoted by J. Black, 'Naval power and British foreign policy in the age of Pitt the Elder', in Black and Woodfine, eds, *British Navy and the Use of Naval Power*, 101.

6. J.G. Coad, *The Royal Dockyards 1690–1850* (Scolar Press, 1989), 315–37; R. Pares, *War and Trade in the West Indies 1739–1763* (Oxford, 1936), 265–325; E. Taillemite, 'Une bataille de l'Atlantique au XVIIIe Siècle: la guerre de Succession d'Autriche, 1744–1748', in *Guerres et Paix 1660–1815*, 133; J. Gwyn, 'The Royal Navy in North America 1712-1776', in Black and Woodfine, eds, *British Navy and the Use of Naval Power*, 139–40.

7. R. Morriss, *The Royal Dockyards during the Revolutionary and Napoleonic Wars* (Leicester, 1983), 44; J.P. Merino, 'Graving Docks in France and spain before 1800', *Mariner's Mirror*, 71 (1985), 48–9.

8. P.H. Boulle, 'Patterns of French Colonial Trade and the Seven Years' War', *Social History, Histoire Sociale*, 7 (1974), 50; J. Meyer, 'The second hundred years' war (1689-1815),' in D. Johnson, F. Bédarida, and F. Crouzet, eds, *Britain and France. Ten Centuries* (London, 1980), 141.

9. D.A. Baugh, 'Why did Britain lose command of the sea during the war for America?', in Black and Woodfine, eds, *British Navy and the Use of Naval Power*, 149–70.

10. Meyer, 'Second hundred years' war', *Britain and France*, 152; R.J.B. Knight, 'The Building and Maintenance of the British Fleet during the Anglo-French Wars 1688–1815', in M. Acerra, J. Merino, and J. Meyer, eds, *Les Marines de Guerre Européennes XVII-XVIIIe Siècles* (Paris, 1985), 35–50; J. Meyer and M. Acerra, 'La Marine française vue par elle-même (XVIIe-XVIIIe siècles)', *Guerres et Paix 1660-1815*, 240.

11. See also Black, 'The British Navy and British Foreign Policy in the first half of the eighteenth century,' in J.M. Black and K.W. Schweizer, eds, *Essays in European History in honour of Ragnhild Hatton* (Lennoxville, 1985), 147–8.

12. Public Record Office, War Office Correspondence 6/7, Dundas to Murray, Private, 23 August 1793.

13. M. Duffy, 'The Foundations of British Naval Power', in Duffy, ed., *The Military Revolution and the State 1500-1800* (Exeter, 1980), 70, 82.

14. J. Pritchard, *Louis XV's Navy 1748-1762. A Study of Organisation and Administration* (Kingston, Ontario, 1987), 81-2; O.Anderson, 'The Establishment of British Supremacy at Sea and the Exchange of Naval Prisoners of War, 1689–1783', *English Historical Review*, 75 (1960), 77–89.

15. See in particular N. Rodger, *The Wooden World. An Anatomy of the Georgian Navy* (London, 1986), Ch. 4–6, and M. Rediker, *Between the Devil and the Deep Blue Sea: Merchant Seamen, Pirates, and the Anglo-American Maritime World, 1700–1750* (Cambridge, 1987).

Introduction

16. J.S. Bromley, ed., *The Manning of the Royal Navy. Selected public pamphlets 1693–1873* (NRS, vol.119, 1974), xxxviii, 245–6, 279; C.J. Bartlett, *Great Britain and Sea Power 1815–1853* (Oxford, 1963), 306–10.
17. Meyer, 'Second hundred years' war,' in Johnson *et. al.*, *Britain and France*, 146.
18. Both Rodger, *The Wooden World*, 203, and S. Gradish, *The Manning of the British Navy during the Seven Years' War* (London, 1980), 111, support the 1755–63 figure; J. Bromley, 'Second hundred years' war', in Johnson *et. al.*, *Britain and France*, 165.
19. Rodger, *Wooden World*, 203.
20. C. Lloyd and J.L.S. Coulter, *Medicine and the Navy 1200–1900*, vol. III, *1714–1815* (London, 1961), 137, 325, 328; C. Lloyd, ed., *The Health of Seamen* (NRS, vol. 107, 1965), 149.
21. Baugh, 'Why did Britain lose command of the sea during the war for America?' in Black and Woodfine, eds, *British Navy and the Use of Naval Power*, 155–6.
22. G. Symcox, *The Crisis of French Naval Power, 1689-1697* (The Hague, 1974); Pritchard, *Louis XV's Navy*; J.R. Dull, *The French Navy and American Independence: A Study of Arms and Diplomacy, 1774–1787* (Princeton, 1975); J.R. Dull, 'Why did the French Revolutionary Navy Fail?' *Proceedings of the Consortium on Revolutionary Europe* (1989) vol. 2, 121–37.
23. Though D.A. Baugh, *British Naval Administration in the Age of Walpole* (Princeton, 1965), 452-93, shows the British navy nevertheless had financial problems too. For on overview see J. Brewer, *The Sinews of Power. War, money and the English state, 1688-1783* (London, 1989).
24. Bartlett, *Great Britain and Sea Power*, 13–21, 88-95, 128–47; A. Lambert, *The Last Sailing Battlefleet. Maintaining Naval Mastery 1815–1850* (London, 1991), 7–8, 13–16.
25. Pritchard, *Louis XV's Navy*, Ch. 1,2 and pp.209–10.

THE BIRTH OF THE IMPERIAL NAVY? ASPECTS OF ENGLISH NAVAL STRATEGY c.1650–90

David Davies

Historians have expended much time and effort in recent years in rediscovering and reinterpreting many of the old truisms of what might be termed classical navalist principles. The navy is now rightly seen once again as an 'instrument of policy', to borrow Sir Herbert Richmond's famous phrase; several historians, notably Paul Kennedy for the whole period of British naval history and Daniel Baugh, Jeremy Black, John Hattendorf, and J. R. Jones for the eighteenth century, have sought to explore the relationship between naval strategy and national policy.[1] Though their claims for the influence of seapower on events are more modest than those made by their predecessors at the turn of the century, paying due deference to the continental aspects of British policy,[2] they still produce a picture of a navy which was always one of the decisive factors, and at certain times *the* decisive factor, in both policy making and in the success or failure of those policies. Indeed, some historians have adopted an interpretation which turns Richmond's formulation on its head, arguing that, in certain circumstances, policy was the instrument of the navy—in other words, that the very existence of a large and capable fleet tempted political leaders to take certain policy decisions which could not have been contemplated otherwise.[3] The possession of such a fleet also led to the evolution of the so-called 'blue water' strategy, which can be summarised in a grossly over-simplified form as a belief that Britain in wartime should forsake continental commitments and confine itself to naval operations, which, it was believed, would be sufficient to defend against invasion and to defeat the enemy (invariably France) by blockade and commerce raiding.[4]

English Naval Strategy c.1650–90

Most of these recent surveys of policy and strategy have concentrated on the so-called 'second hundred years war' after 1689. Unfortunately, this emphasis has perpetuated (albeit unconsciously) a particularly rigid example of historical tunnel vision: the all-embracing chapter headings entitled 'the Dutch wars' and 'the French wars' which recur endlessly in naval and more general histories. Jeremy Black, for one, has reminded us of the dangers of over-generalization by demolishing the notion of a 'second hundred years war', noting that at least fifteen years of that period were actually spent in close alliance with France.[5] Similarly, the notion that virtually the entire naval history of the period 1650–88 can be seen purely in terms of conflict with the Dutch, still regarded (consciously or unconsciously) as a peculiar aberration in the list of England's 'natural enemies', dangerously obscures a more complex picture. As a result, several misconceptions have grown up about the origins of the naval strategy implemented after 1688, and one aim of this paper is to provide a rather broader context for some of the measures taken in the early stages of William III's French war. In order to do this, several themes need to be considered, particularly with regard to the 1660s and 1670s: the nature and strategic potential of the navy itself, and the principles which underpinned naval strategy, particularly with regard to the three main causes of concern which dominated strategic thinking in the decades before the French wars began, namely the Dutch, the French, and the Mediterranean.

Historians have long recognised the crucial importance of the creation of the republic in 1649 in transforming the nature and role of the navy. The urgent need to defend the infant regime against attack from the many European monarchies which might have chosen to support the Stuarts led to an immediate and impressive strengthening of the fleet, which doubled in size in the three years after Charles I's execution and continued to expand at a remarkable rate throughout the 1650s.[6] By 1664, when Charles II embarked on his first war with the Dutch, the fleet which he had available to him (much of it the product of the Interregnum building programmes) was three times the size of the force which his father had lost to parliament in 1642 (Table 1).

Table 1

NOMINAL STRENGTH OF THE NAVY, 1618–1685

Rate of ship	1618	1642	1664	1685
First	4	3	4	9
Second	8	13	13	14
Third	4	10	15	39
Fourth	3	3	42	42
Fifth	2	2	31	12
Sixth	2	4	13	9
Royal yachts	-	-	8	18

Note:

The size of ships in each rate, and the amount of ordnance carried, both increased considerably during the course of the century, and the system of rating itself was not finalised until the 1650s. Therefore, these figures are intended for comparison only, and have been gained by transposing the later ratings onto the earlier years. *Sources:* A.P. McGowan, ed., *The Jacobin Commissions of Enquiry: 1608 and 1618* (N[avy] R[ecords] S[ociety], 1971) 258, for 1618; J.R. Powell and E.K. Timings, eds, *Documents relating to the Civil War 1642–8*, (NRS, 1963) 7–8, for 1642; F. Fox, *Great Ships: the Battlefleet of King Charles II* (1980), 183 for 1664 and 1695.

The nature of the ships, and the tactics which they adopted, changed too. The tendency to place more guns on the broadside encouraged the development of the 'line of battle', first used at the battle of the Gabbard in 1653, and the more constant, close range bombardments which resulted encouraged the substitution of large, heavily armed and purpose-built warships in place of the hired merchantmen which had formed a substantial part of the fleet in Elizabethan and early Stuart times.[7] With their new fleet of powerful warships, the republican governments soon switched to a more aggressive strategy, waging war on the Netherlands and Spain, intervening with substantial naval forces in the Mediterranean and the Baltic, and maintaining a belligerent posture which impressed and alarmed heads of state from Russia to Morocco—a naval grand strategy which 'blue water' polemicists of the eighteenth century were to see as a blueprint and ideal for their own day.[8]

In fact, the strategic principles underlying the naval expansion of the 1650s owed a great deal to the past. Defence against invasion, of course, has always been the main function of the English navy, and as Bernard Capp has recently pointed out, many of the apparently aggressive strategic decisions taken in the 1650s, such as the decision to go to war with Spain, were often born out of the insecure, defensive mentality of the regime—in this case, going to war with either France or Spain ensured that they would not combine against England. Even Cromwell's use of the fleet on a global scale reveals strong echoes of Elizabethan and early Stuart strategy: the attacks on Spain's Caribbean possessions and her plate fleets were undertaken for much the same mixture of geopolitical and financial motives which had characterised Drake's more ambitious operations, while the activities of Blake's fleet in the Mediterranean, especially his operations against the Barbary corsairs, harked back to the crown's abortive attacks on Algiers in 1620 and Salée in 1637.[9] What made the 1650s different was that the fleet was finally large

16

enough to enable such operations to be carried out regularly and effectively, an effectiveness enhanced by English superiority (or improved technology) in the fields of gunnery, ship design, and tactics.

The restored monarchy maintained the 'big navy' policy of the republic. Indeed, the years after the Restoration also witnessed a marked switch to a 'big ship' policy: construction was concentrated on the first to third rates, the backbone of the line of battle, and the numbers of fourth to sixth rates, which were more directly useful for commerce protection, declined markedly (see Table 1 above). This change came about both because Charles II and his brother James, the Lord High Admiral, preferred big ships (as their father had done) as more fitting symbols of the monarchy's power, but also because of the impact of the new line tactics, which demanded larger, more heavily armed and more 'survivable' warships.[10] In turn, this new dominance of the 'line-of-battle ships' also helped to dictate naval strategy in the period 1650–90 in a way which will be considered more fully later in this paper, but which can be summarised briefly here as meaning that the largest possible fleet of the largest warships would seek out and destroy the enemy battlefleet, thereby securing command of the seas. This preponderance of the larger rates caused such problems in the 1690s, when the French perversely refused to send their battlefleet to sea and chose instead to raid English maritime commerce, that the emphasis of the English naval shipbuilding programme had to be modified to allow for the building of more fourth to sixth rates.[11]

The interpretation presented so far of the changing balance of the fleet and the changing tactics might suggest a neglect of one of the other great constant tasks of the British navy, namely the protection of trade. Indeed, it will be seen later in this paper that the Dutch wars *did* witness a conscious strategic decision to forsake the direct protection of overseas trade, but at the time there seemed to be powerful arguments far taking such a potentially dangerous course. There is also ample evidence to show that in the long periods of peace between and after the Dutch wars, successive regimes developed a much more formal and thorough strategy for protecting British coastal and overseas trade—notably the evolution of convoy systems, the establishment of a 'western squadron' to guard trade entering and leaving the Channel, and the near-permanent stationing of a fleet in the Mediterranean to guard British merchant vessels there.[12] By the 1660s and 1670s, then, England had the most powerful navy it had ever possessed, with the recent examples of the successful, aggressive maritime strategy (as it was perceived) of the Interregnum regimes to provide a role model for its use. Indeed, in one respect the opportunities presented by the navy at this time might seem to be even greater. Whereas the regimes of the 1650s, like those after

1689, possessed the large armies which could present a government with the constant dilemma of choosing between maritime and continental strategies, the monarchy of Charles II did not possess an army large enough to allow it to undertake sustained, large scale continental operations. Therefore, it could be argued that the years between 1660 and 1689 constituted the only period when England had the means to implement a classical 'blue water' strategy, *and* lacked the distraction of a large army which could encourage the adoption of alternative strategies.

For those who made naval strategy, the period before 1689 presented other opportunities which did not exist in the following period. The infrequency of parliamentary sessions, the censorship imposed after the Restoration, and the absence of a credible alternative policy, all ensured that strategy was less an object for public debate than it became in later years.[13] Strategy was decided in secret, by the king, the lord high admiral, and their chief ministers, working through and obtaining advice from such formal bodies as the privy council's committee for foreign affairs or (after 1673) the board of Admiralty, and informal bodies such as the ad hoc committees of senior officers who advised Charles II in the second Dutch war. Indeed, on several occasions in the second and third wars Charles and James brought all their strategic advisors together, going to the fleet themselves, accompanied by several senior ministers, in order to attend councils of war with the captains and admirals.[14] Parliament did discuss naval strategy on several occasions, but never in a consistent or particularly coherent manner. Moreover, such debates were invariably retrospective investigations of the miscarriages of previous campaigns, not constructive alternative programmes for the future, and were also only parts of more general attacks on unpopular ministers. In 1667–8, for example, the parliamentary investigation into the miscarriages of the second Dutch war criticised the failure to follow up the victory at Lowestoft in 1665, the abortive attack on the Dutch East Indies fleet at Bergen in the same campaign, and the division of the fleet in both 1666 and 1667, but these charges were made with the benefit of hindsight and were designed to undermine the position of the lord high admiral, James, duke of York, of his father-in-law Clarandon, and of several other ministers.[15] Similarly, in 1674 the question of the responsibility for ordering the attack on the Dutch Smyrna fleet two years earlier, the incident which opened the third war in earnest, was raised in the context of parliamentary attacks on Buckingham and Arlington, the two ministers perceived as being most responsible for an unpopular war. The king and his ministers might have had to face a parliamentary inquisition *after* a naval war, but not a running public commentary on their choice of strategy *during* that war.

In these circumstances, strategy could be made in great secrecy. In 1683, for example, Lord Dartmouth's fleet (which was actually intended to evacuate and demolish the English colony at Tangier) was reported variously to be sailing to intercept the Spanish plate fleet, to escort a French squadron out of the Baltic, to monitor the movements of the Dutch fleet, to attack Salée in Morocco, to establish a new colony at Mamora in north Africa, to carry a doctor of civil law to Spain to persuade the governor of Cadiz to salute English warships, or to undertake a survey of the Channel Islands.[16] The very fact that all of these objectives were considered in informed circles to be quite plausible is in itself an indication both of an awareness of the potential of the fleet which England now possessed, and of the secrecy which shaped the making both of naval strategy and of the country's foreign policy as a whole.

In their assessment of national policy in the decades after 1650, particularly with regard to the Dutch, historians have recently started to move away from a purely 'commercial' interpretation to stress that conflict over trade co-existed with ideological divisions which also caused tension between England and the Netherlands.[17] If this is so, and given that naval strategy invariably implements and therefore reflects the aims of national policy, one would expect the use made of the navy to reveal a similar combination of commercial and ideological elements. For Sir Herbert Richmond, the strategy of the Dutch wars was relatively straightforward: England 'had to attain such a superiority at sea that it would be possible continuously to maintain a position off the Dutch ports', although 'the principal object ... remained undefined. Whether it was the capture of shipping or the destruction of the main body of the enemy was never completely defined'.[18] Even with this note of caution, Richmond's interpretation suggests a strategy which was based on logical and rational foundations, if not always consistent ones, and this impression is reinforced by his dismissal of what would have seemed, to the eyes of a twentieth century admiral, to have been the most illogical and irrational ingredient of seventeenth century naval policy, namely the English claim to the sovereignty of the seas.[19] Richmond would probably have concurred with the mystified reaction of Sir Edward Nicholas, former secretary of state, to the news in 1667 that the duke of York had given his new son, at that time the likely next or next-but-one king of England, the name of Edgar, after the Saxon king who had supposedly first asserted sovereignty over the British seas.[20] If the Lord High Admiral seemed to abandon rationality when naming his son, then perhaps his naval strategy was also rather less calculated than Richmond assumed.

Those who directed naval strategy between 1650 and 1690 certainly recognised the potential of the fleet they had created. English naval strategy in all three of the Dutch wars hinged on massing the largest possible fleet in the North Sea: all other considerations were secondary to this end. Squadrons were withdrawn from overseas stations, with English merchants there being told explicitly 'that they [should] look to themselves'.[21] Only when the campaigning season was over, usually in late September or October, were convoys and squadrons sent to the Mediterranean or further afield, and even then their despatch hinged on the likelihood of their being back in time for the next summer's campaign.[22] Preventing a dissipation of forces could be justified on several theoretical grounds, but it was also conditioned by experience— the English defeat at the battle of Dungeness in October 1652, the first major engagement of the Dutch wars was attributed chiefly to the detachment of a squadron to the Mediterranean, and thereafter all commanders-in-chief were determined not to weaken their main fleet.[23] Therefore, the principle of English naval strategy in all the Dutch wars seemed clear enough. The largest battlefleet was to inflict a rapid and crushing defeat on the Dutch: if this was achieved, the short-term risk of abandoning trade and the colonies would have been justified. However, this 'grand fleet' strategy begged the obvious question of just how the Dutch were to be defeated, and it was in this respect that the apparent clarity of purpose underlying strategy was submerged beneath a conglomeration of often contradictory or unrealistic objectives.

The importance of destroying Dutch trade was recognised clearly enough. The famous remark of Pepys's merchant friend Captain George Cocke, 'that the trade of the world is too little for us two, therefore one must down' has been quoted many times, but it was echoed by others in positions of more authority: in 1672, for instance, the earl of Shaftesbury remarked that 'he that can trade best, will carry on the war longest'.[24] Broadly speaking, there seemed to be two ways of destroying Dutch trade. If their main fleet could be engaged and destroyed, the English navy could maintain a blockade of the Dutch coast and roam at will over the North Sea, mopping up whatever Dutch trade remained at sea and rapidly forcing the enemy to seek a humiliating and (from the English viewpoint) highly lucrative peace treaty. The other method involved attacking Dutch commerce first, particularly their very rich Smyrna and East Indies convoys as they returned to the Netherlands.[25] In turn, this strategy might also achieve the other end, namely drawing the Dutch fleet to sea to protect the returning merchantmen. Much of the unsatisfactory nature of the Dutch wars, from the contemporary English point of view, stemmed from the failure to apply one strategy consistently: fleets were shifted constantly from one goal to another, depending on whichever short term objective was being pursued at the time. In 1665, for example, the fleet went to to sea with the twin objectives of capturing the great merchant convoys after they had gone 'northabout' round Scotland, and provoking the Dutch main fleet into coming to sea for a decisive engagement. In order to achieve both ends simultaneously the fleet was to cruise about twelve leagues north-west of the Texel, roughly on the latitude of 55½ degrees north. In fact, the attempt to hold this station was bedevilled by bad weather, a shortage of victuals, poor intelligence of Dutch movements and finally by the decision to move northwards to intercept the Dutch East Indies fleet as it ran for home along the coast of Norway—even though, as the Lord High Admiral himself recognised, this move left the English coast completely open if the Dutch main fleet came out.[26] Similarly, in 1672 the strategic debate centred on whether to blockade the Dutch coast and attempt a landing, or to sweep the seas in search of yet another East Indies fleet.[27]

This strategic confusion stemmed from the fact that the destruction of Dutch trade, and even the defeat of the Dutch state, was not just an end in itself. The 'Elizabethan' notion of a self-financing naval war remained very attractive, especially to the almost permanently impoverished Interregnum and Restoration regimes, and this idea gained even more currency in the 1650s, when the fleet captured perhaps 1,500 Dutch prizes in the war of 1652–4 and subsequently intercepted Spanish plate convoys on two occasions.[28] The new fleet could therefore be seen as a gigantic privateering squadron, winning untold riches for its owner, the state. The court embarked on the second Dutch war in 1664 believing confidently that it would save a large part of the parliamentary vote of £2,500,000, and would then make a huge profit out of Dutch prizes and a punitive peace; individual officers volunteered for service in the expectation of personal gain from prize money; and in 1666 the duke of Albemarle even advocated immediate declarations of war against France and Denmark, on the grounds that waiting for them to declare war on England would lose several weeks' opportunities for capturing many valuable prizes.[29] In this respect, then, English war policy was based on avarice, and naval strategy reflected this. When the fleet moved north to intercept the Dutch East Indies fleet in 1665, it was in the belief that the escorting flagship was carrying two chests of gold and the vice-admiral three more, and when it was learned that they had taken refuge in the neutral harbour of Bergen the duke of York ordered that 'if a fair opportunity offer itself of doing any service upon them, I desire you would not neglect it out of any scrupulous consideration of that port in which they lie', regardless of the fact, as already noted, that sending the fleet to Norway effectively left the English coast defenceless.[30] After the attack on Bergen was ignominiously repulsed by the Dutch and Danes, James justified it on the grounds that 'the value of the ships to be seized was considerable enough to make it fit to run some hazard'.[31]

Regardless of the lessons of Bergen, the makers of English strategy continued to be obsessed with the idea of capturing the Smyrna or East Indies fleets. The campaign of 1672 saw a particularly heated debate on strategy, with several lengthy discussions at the committee for foreign affairs and several visits by Charles, James, and their ministers to the fleet to discuss strategy with their admirals.[32] The strategy of the third Dutch war was complicated further by the addition of a new objective, the seizure of Dutch towns and islands which would be ceded permanently to England when, as expected, the French army overran the republic. The first war in the 1650s had not witnessed any amphibious or land-based operations, but the success of Sir Robert Holmes's raid on Westerschelling in 1666, coupled, perhaps, with a desire not to let the French have all the glory on land, led to serious attempts in both 1672 and 1673 to prepare a landing in Zealand. Regardless of the debatable realism of the proposed invasion, which was to culminate in the captured towns being offered the chance to send MPs to Westminster,[33] it immediately imposed another constraint on strategic planning. For any landing to be successful, the fleet would have to lie close to the Dutch shore for some considerable period of time, leading to a failure to intercept their trade in the open sea, while the invasion strategy still begged the question of whether or not to destroy the main Dutch fleet first. Charles prevaricated, the preparation of the invasion army degenerated into low farce, the old problems of weather and victuals prevented the fleet from holding its station off the Dutch coast for long enough, and the inhabitants of Flushing and other Zealand towns were spared the dubious pleasure of enjoying 'all privileges that any native Englishman does, and not to be taxed but by consent in parliament'.[34]

The Zealand invasion plan represents one example of one of the other guiding concerns of Restoration naval strategy, the defence and advancement of national 'reputation' and 'honour'. This concern took several forms. A forward, aggressive strategy was essential, not only for its own sake, (as a means towards the ends of victory and profit), but in order to enhance the reputation of the king of England both at home and abroad, and any reverse therefore had to be avenged as quickly as possible.[35] This attitude squared comfortably with the outlooks of the naval officers, who usually shared identical views about their own 'reputation' and 'honour'. Imputations of misconduct could lead to duels between accuser and accused to bitter accusations traded for years on end, or to a suicidally reckless urge to clear one's name in the next battle—as in the case of Vice-Admiral Sir William Berkeley, publicly accused of cowardice in 1665 and meeting his death in 1666 by sailing too far ahead of his own fleet in order to get at the enemy first.[36] On one level, several of the naval battles of the second and third Dutch wars were simply the arenas in which old adversaries tried to settle old scores, either with their own side or with the enemy: the course of the battle of the Texel in August 1673 was largely determined by the decision of the admiral of the blue squadron, Sir Edward Spragge, to seek out at all costs his old enemy, Admiral van Tromp, thereby abandoning any pretence of sticking to a prearranged strategic plan.[37]

This image of the navy as the most potent symbol, and main upholder, of national honour, was not apparent only in wartime. The English claim to the sovereignty of the so-called 'British Seas', asserted most vigorously by John Selden in his 'Mare Clausum' of 1635, was taken up both by the republic and the restored monarchy, but both regimes (unlike that of Charles I, which had first made a concerted attempt to enforce such sovereignty) possessed the naval strength to make the claim effective.[38] When the first formal set of general instructions was issued to captains in 1663, the twenty-second article specified that foreign vessels should strike their topsails and take in their flags when meeting an English warship in the 'British seas', defined as extending from Stadtland in Norway to Cape Finisterre. It they failed to do so, captains were to use their 'utmost endeavour to compel them thereunto and in no wise to suffer any dishonour to be done to his majesty'. Even outside those seas, English warships were never to strike their colours first.[39] Not surprisingly, these provisions led to an unending series of quarrels and diplomatic incidents with virtually every maritime power in Europe. In 1647, a full scale battle took place between a Swedish convoy and some English ships, while in 1683 an English warship was forced to salute at Cadiz after being surrounded by an entire Spanish fleet, an incident which led to talk both of war with Spain and of the execution of the captain for having given in, even to overwhelming odds.[40] These were only some of the more spectacular instances. On a voyage in the Mediterranean in 1673, for instance, Captain Charles Wylde refused to salute Malta because it was 'a den of thieves', and also threatened to bombard Messina.[41] Two years later, his colleague Captain Joseph Harris was sentenced to death for striking his colours, and reprieved only when the muskets were at his head.[42] Naval captains who enforced the salute, and English diplomats abroad who attempted to mend the damage caused by the captains, knew that the sovereignty of the seas and the salute to the flag were not vague notions which demanded only lip service.

If the 'salute to the flag' could easily have led to war with virtually any state at any time, a scenario prevented only by the exigencies of foreign policy-making at a higher level, then it could easily form the pretext when England *did* decide to go to war. Regardless of their long term causes, two of the three Dutch wars began with incidents over the salute.

The first war began when the Dutch failed to salute Blake in the English Channel, the third when they failed to salute the tiny royal yacht *Merlin*, an incident which had been engineered deliberately by Charles and James to provide the excuse for declaring war. Moreover, the English agenda at every post-war peace conference invariably included recognition of their right to the salute, with the Dutch attempting to insert a much narrower definition of the 'British seas' and to prevent such occurrences as the *Merlin* incident by ensuring that whole fleets did not have to salute single English ships.[43] In fact, the English position on the salute was never as confident as it seemed. In 1661, the duke of York asked his advisors 'what hath been the common practice about making of forrayne ships to strike sail to us', and there were several subsequent attempts to collect precedents on the subject.[44] York's own secretary, Sir William Coventry, had serious reservations about the whole question, believing it was not worth fighting a war over,[45] and this view was also advanced by Sir Philip Meadowes in his tract 'Observations Concerning the Dominion and Sovereignty of the Seas'. Meadowes probably wrote this work in the 1670s, presenting it to the king in 1687 and eventually publishing it in 1689: in it, he made the obvious point that the claim to the salute would lead England into constant conflict with other nations, while a failure to enforce it would destroy the king's reputation at home.[46] On the other hand, Coventry and Meadowes were probably in a minority in their own time. The works published on the subject throughout the period unanimously supported the claim to the sovereignty of the seas, and some were even prepared to go well beyond the official position—Sir Henry Shere, a close friend of Samuel Pepys, advocated the creation of a 'maritime monarchy' which would give England sovereignty over the entire ocean.[47] In private, Charles and James probably inclined more towards Shere than Meadowes. Certainly, the acquisition of Tangier in 1661 led to confident talk at court for many years of an overseas empire and of England becoming a great power in the Mediterranean:[48] the new navy allowed the crown to dream of maritime supremacy and colonial dominion, even if the emptiness of the exchequer would not allow those dreams to become reality.

If we accept that Charles and James were serious about the sovereignty of the seas, about their own and their country's 'reputation', and about the potential and importance of their navy, then questions need to be asked about their relationship with France. Historians have made many assumptions about Charles II's relationship with Louis XIV, but central to these is a belief that Charles was not prepared to go to war with France, and that on the whole he trusted Louis.[49] These assumptions are based on the standard diplomatic, personal, and related sources, which do provide a detailed insight into the making of policy, but not necessarily into the implementation of that policy—in other words, into the question of what the English and French fleets actually did, and why.

In the 1660s, inspired by Colbert as minister of marine, France embarked on a rapid and impressive programme of naval construction. Regardless of their own friendly feelings towards France, Charles and James immediately perceived this as a potential threat, the latter believing by the end of 1668 that French naval expansion posed the greatest threat to England.[50] This lesson had been reinforced during the second Dutch war, which France had joined on the Dutch side at the start of 1666. Contemporaries recognized full well that the prevailing winds and tides, together with the size and power of the French navy, meant that invasion (particularly a preliminary invasion of Ireland) was a far greater threat in a French war than in a Dutch war. If the naval administration needed to learn the lesson, it was contained in the tracts of the Elizabethan and early Stuart admiral Sir William Monson, which were circulating in manuscript in the 1660s and which gained great credit with Pepys, at least, because of Monson's seemingly uncanny prediction of the Dutch attack on the Medway in 1667.[51] Throughout 1666 and 1667, the ministry and the country genuinely feared invasion from France, and particular attention was devoted to the defence of Ireland.[52] Concern over the French threat also manifested itself in the notorious 'division of the fleet' in 1666, when a squadron was detached from the main fleet in the North Sea to intercept a French force sailing into the Channel to rendezvous with the Dutch. The intelligence of this force proved false, and the division meant that the weakened English fleet was badly mauled in the subsequent 'four days battle' with the Dutch, but the court and ministry had genuinely believed in the danger.[53] Thereafter in the 1666 and 1667 campaigns, neither the English nor the French navies behaved in a way which suggests two protagonists who were deliberately holding back from each other. The English fleet spent much of September 1666 in a vain attempt to find and engage the French, and in a hot fight the powerful new French second rate *Rubis* was captured, subsequently joining the English fleet as the *French Ruby*.[54] Other, equally bitter, single ship actions took place in the West Indies, emphasising the point that France posed a greater threat in that theatre than the Dutch—indeed, Charles and James responded by sending out a force of one third rate, seven fourths and two sixths under Sir John Harman, the only large English naval squadron sent to the West Indies between the 1650s and 1690s.[55]

The French war of 1666–7 taught several uncomfortable lessons. The ease with which French warships outran English ones, and the impressive sailing qualities of the *French Ruby*, indicated that French

25

warships were superior, in many respects, to English ones: they were larger, faster, and more manouevrable, with fewer but heavier guns.[56] Moreover, English strategy in a French war would clearly need to be different. In 1666, an 'advertisement' evocatively entitled 'That our Misfortunes at Sea do happen by Carrying on the War in the Wrong Place' had identified the cornerstone of French strategy, and had proposed a solution which, in turn, anticipates one of the cornerstones of eighteenth-century English strategy: 'we see that Brest is our enemy's great frontier ... that he lies free to the western ocean, and can presently be out ... and that by lying so near unto the chops of the channel, our trade both out and home, is in a manner at his mercy'. Therefore, Brest would need to be blockaded by fleets operating, in the author's opinion, from Kinsale and Cork.[57]

The next naval confrontation with France occurred soon afterwards. In 1668, England prepared a fleet for sea as its commitment to the 'Triple Alliance', the diplomatic structure intended to compel Louis XIV to an acceptable settlement of his war with Spain. The events of 1668 have usually been dismissed by historians as a sham, with Charles II opposed to any war with France, with parliament voting too little money to set out a proper fleet, and with Louis in any case outmaneouvring his opponents by signing a treaty on his own terms: Charles's most recent biographer calls the naval deployment in 1668 'no more-than a parade of a small force'.[58] In fact, by the end of May 1668 a powerful fleet was either at sea or being made ready, a fleet comprising one first rate, seven seconds, seventeen thirds, twenty-one fourths, and four fifths.[59] Why such a great force, if Charles II did not perceive a threat from France? Firstly, there was genuine concern about French naval preparations and the danger of invasion;[60] secondly, having a large fleet actually at sea allowed Charles to keep every option open, as well as giving him a very real and apparent diplomatic lever on Louis. To use the jargon of modern naval warfare, Charles was implementing a strategy of 'flexible response'. The instructions to his admiral, Sir Thomas Allin, also reveal some interesting strategic insights. Allin's station was off Land's End and in the Soundings, to cover potential French moves into the Channel or against Ireland—a correct assessment of the nature of the French naval threat as revealed in 1666–7. If Allin found that the French greatly exceeded him in strength, he was to withdraw up the Channel to the Downs, a strategy which seems remarkably similar to the notion of the 'fleet in being', supposedly first formulated by Arthur Herbert, earl of Torrington, when retreatinig in the face of a superior French fleet in 1690; indeed, Herbert was one of the captains serving under Allin off Land's End in the summer of 1668.[61]

After 1668, England and France began the series of convoluted diplomatic negotiations which eventually culminated in the secret treaty of Dover and the combined Anglo-French attack on the Netherlands in 1672. Despite the new alliance, however, Charles and James remained suspicious of the French naval build-up. The king tried unsuccessfully in the treaty negotiations to persuade Louis to suspend his building programme, and although Charles stressed his desire for close naval cooperation with the French throughout the war, he had some private doubts, believing that the French were not up to the more difficult operations and that they should not be informed of England's plans for invading Zealand.[62] The smug belief in French incompetence at sea seemed to be confirmed by their failure to employ their squadron effectively at the battle of the Texel in August 1673, but such smugness was misplaced. Even during the war, siren voices warned that the French were using the opportunity to learn the English method of fighting at sea, as well as finding out about the harbours and coasts of England against the day when they would have to invade it.[63] After Charles II's precipitate withdrawal from the war, French naval successes in the Mediterranean and further examples of the ease with which French warships could outrun English ones when trying to avoid giving the 'salute to the flag' all seemed to confirm the threat which Louis XIV now posed at sea.[64] In 1675 and 1677, therefore, the ministry went to parliament in an attempt to obtain the money for a huge new construction programme to keep pace with French building, a programme which eventually settled on one first rate, nine seconds, and twenty thirds. Despite backbench doubts about what Charles might do with the money, fear of France won the day, and the necessary funds were voted. As two opponents of the crown, Thomas Clarges and William Garraway, put it in the House on 6 March 1677, 'the king of France's great fleet is not built to take Vienna...he knows not what he has else to conquer but us'.[65]

The new building programme was only in its very early stages when, at the end of 1677, England began to prepare once again for war with France. As in 1668, the policy (promoted above all by Lord Treasurer Danby) was designed to force Louis to accept moderate terms to conclude a war, this time with the Dutch, and as with the events of 1668, historians have long debated the question of just how far Charles was prepared to go towards war with France.[66] The naval mobilization undertaken in 1678 casts some interesting light on this question. Serious planning for the French war began in December 1677, with a meeting on the twentieth attended by the duke of York, Danby, the duke of Monmouth (Captain-General of the army), Sir Joseph Williamson and Henry Coventry (the two secretaries of state), and Sir Thomas Chicheley (master of the ordnance). Those present immediately stated their aware-

27

ness of the differences between a French war and one against the Dutch, noting, for example, that the French could mount a serious naval threat even in winter. Consequently, a proposal was adopted to keep the great ships manned and equipped for the whole winter, a radical departure from past precedent, but a move which foreshadowed an identical, disastrous experiment in 1692. Squadrons of fifty ships of the line were to be maintained both in the Channel and the Mediterranean, with the Dutch providing half the strength of each force. A decision had already been taken by the Admiralty board to use Port Mahon and Lisbon to support the projected Mediterranean fleet, an augmented version of the large squadron already operating under Sir John Narbrough against the corsairs of Algiers.[67] By the end of January a meeting of parliament, which would be required to vote money for the war, was imminent, and the administration had ready more detailed plans for the disposition of an English naval contribution of ninety major ships (Table 2).[68]

Table 2

PLAN FOR THE SUMMER FLEET, 28 JANUARY 1678

Station	Rate of ship						Total	Fire-ships	Lesser craft
	1	2	3	4	5	6			
Mediterranean	1	2	6	16	-	-	25	5	15
Channel	3	3	8	11	-	-	25	5	32
West Indies	-	-	2	10	3	-	15	2	2
Northward	-	-	-	2	4	4	10	-	-
Soundings, etc.	-	-	-	3	4	3	10	-	-
St Helena	-	-	-	5	-	-	5	-	1

Despite the worries of some MPs that Charles would use any money they voted to impose absolute monarchy rather than to set out the fleet, the House of Commons voted on 14 February to supply the £108,840 a month necessary to maintain the ninety ships.[69]

In February, too, a series of meetings took place between English naval administrators and officers on the one hand, and Cornelis Evertsen, the Dutch admiral and envoy, on the other. The main issue, the numbers of ships to be supplied by each nation, was discussed on the seventeenth, and revealed some differences of opinion. Evertsen agreed on a Dutch force in the Mediterranean of eighteen major and six minor vessels to complement England's proposed twenty-five ships, but suggested that the Dutch should take the main responsibility for the northern seas and for convoy duties. Charles objected, insisting that the Dutch should supply at least twenty ships in the Channel and that each country should guard its own interests to the northward. A private memorandum on this meeting by secretary of state Williamson expressed the English government's doubts about the ability of the Dutch to supply their quota in the

Channel, queried their readiness and their competence, and proposed that Charles should reinforce his own Channel fleet with the ten ships allocated to the northward while insisting that the Dutch northern squadron should come into the Channel in the event of a threatened invasion of England or Ireland.[70] Further meetings in late February and early March dealt with more detailed strategic issues. Frigates and smaller craft were to be stationed off the French coast outside Boulogne, St Valery, Dieppe, Le Havre, St Malo, Ushant, and elsewhere, presumably to act as scouts and to obstruct trade. A force of one third rate and five fourths was to cruise between Cape St Vincent and Cape Spartel. Bases in the Mediterranean were discussed: Port Mahon was agreed on as the main base, with a careening hulk and magazine to be maintained there, but a hulk was also proposed for Puntal, near Cadiz, and Porto Ferraio on Elba was suggested as another potential forward base.[71] Narbrough had already been ordered to collect all English merchant ships from Italy and send them home as quickly as possible, and at the end of March he was given new orders to protect Tangier and Port Mahon, together with assurances that reinforcements, led by the first rate *St Michael*, were on the way.[72]

By the beginning of April, then, the naval war strategy was in place. In the Mediterranean, the combined Anglo-Dutch fleet's first objective, the recapture of Sicily, had already been accomplished by the Spanish, so the fleet was to switch instead 'to form such further designs upon the French in those parts as may be for the good of the common cause', such as engaging the French Mediterranean fleet, blockading Toulon, protecting Catalonia against any French threat, securing Mediterranean trade, cutting off French trade, and generally harrying the French coast 'for the wearying them out of the war'. In the Channel, the combined fleet was to attain command of the seas, disrupt French trade, and generally harass the French coastline.[73] However, the uncertainty surrounding the peace negotiations soon affected the preparation of the fleet. On 31 May all further pressing of seamen was halted, and by mid-June the despatch of the *St Michael* and a second rate to the Mediterranean had been postponed indefinitely, though contingency plans to send these ships if war began were still current as late as the first week of August.[74] Meanwhile, the fleet cruised aimlessly in the Channel, testing the sailing qualities of its new ships and moving back and forth between the Downs and Spithead.[75] By 1 August, virtually the whole of the planned force was at sea. Although the West Indies squadron had not been despatched, the other detached squadrons (together with the larger units intended for the Mediterranean) were still in home waters, and the Dutch had proved very dilatory in getting their ships ready, the total force at sea or almost ready for sea comprised 118 ships of all rates, including five firsts, four seconds, sixteen thirds, and forty fourths, carrying a total of 20,465 men.[76] On 10 August, orders were given to pay off the four largest ships of the Channel fleet, a move which marked the effective end of the 'French war' of 1678, although many of the other ships remained in service until the summer of 1679 because of the government's inability to pay them off.[77]

Plainly, then, if Charles II had never intended to go to war with France in 1678 he had gone to remarkable lengths (and remarkable expense) to preserve the illusion that he would. In one respect, this can again be seen in the context of flexible response—actually having the ships at sea allowed him to respond quickly to any eventuality. However, other actions of his in 1678–9 suggest that his attitude was more complex than this. Even though he had signed a secret treaty with Louis in May 1678, promising to stay neutral, disband his forces, and prorogue parliament, he remained concerned about the French fleet, and over the winter of 1678–9 he authorised several covert operations to obtain intelligence about its strength and preparedness. Ships were sent to ply off the French coast, and two young naval lieutenants were sent undercover to reconnoitre the fortifications of Brest and the ships lying there, though one 'blew his cover' by arriving at Morlaix aboard a naval ketch which had no plausible excuse for being there, and then got into a public argument in the town with the ketch's captain.[78]

The naval mobilization of 1678 is significant in other respects. Historians have tended to assume that England went into the French war in 1689 poorly prepared for its requirements, and that William III foisted on his English admirals a major commitment in the Mediterranean, which they did not want.[79] However, as Sir George Clark noted long ago, the naval war plans implemented in 1689 were only those drawn up in 1678, right down to the ratios of English to Dutch ships and the dispositions of the warships on the different stations, and the war plans of 1678 had been overwhelmingly an English conception.[80] The Mediterranean bases proposed in 1689, Port Mahon and Porto Ferraio, were not forced on the English by the Dutch. They were proposed by the English themselves, presumably relying on the 1678 plans—which could have been drawn either from the papers in the secretary of state's office, or from the memories of those who were close to the planning in both years, such as Danby, Sir John Chicheley (an Admiralty commissioner in 1689, and son to 1678's master of the ordnance), and Arthur Herbert, first commissioner of the Admiralty in 1689 and vice-admiral of the Mediterranean fleet in 1678.[81] Indeed, the notion that the large scale, permanent deployment in the Mediterranean, undertaken by the combined fleets after 1689 was forced by the Dutch onto the unwilling English, is difficult to sustain. Since the days of Blake in the 1650s, successive

30

regimes had maintained an almost permanent naval presence in the Mediterranean in order to fight seemingly endless wars against Algiers, Tunis, Tripoli, and Salée, and in many peacetime years by far the greatest part of the navy's operational strength was to be found in the Mediterranean, not the Channel. Almost all of William III's flag officers, including his first two commanders-in-chief, Herbert and Russell, were men whose naval experience had been gained largely, and in some cases almost exclusively, in the Mediterranean.[82] Shifting alliances, the shifting requirements of wars against different Barbary nations, and the unsuitability of England's own colony at Tangier as a naval base, had meant that English naval captains had made use of, and knew the merits and demerits of, virtually every base they would employ in the French wars after 1689, notably Port Mahon, Lisbon, Livorno, Malta, and significantly, Gibraltar.[83] Thus the navy may have been poorly prepared for war in 1689 in the sense that that changes in the naval administration and the need to liaise with the Dutch delayed the actual setting out of the fleet, but they were certainly well prepared in terms of having a preordained war strategy and a clear perception of the importance of the Mediterranean, even if they did not necessarily agree with William III on the precise timing of a major deployment to that theatre. The 1678 blueprint for a French war certainly was not perfect, in the sense that it placed too much emphasis on the disruption of French maritime trade (of which there was actually very little), too little on the need to establish a new base to the westward to bottle up Brest, and too much on the assumption that the French, like the Dutch, would always attempt to send a battlefleet to sea, but it did provide a basis for Anglo-Dutch naval strategy at the start of the wars of 1689–1713.[84]

Finally, one question remains—did the governments in the second half of the seventeenth century make full use of the fleet they had created? It would be easy to argue that the republic did, as shown by the deployment of large squadrons to the Mediterranean, the West Indies, and the Baltic, but that the restored monarchy did not, largely because it lacked the money to do so. This interpretation would be a little too simplistic. Charles and James might have lacked the money, but they certainly did understand the potential of their navy—in the second Dutch war, for instance, by deploying a squadron to the West Indies, or in the third by planning to deploy forces in the East Indies and the Baltic.[85] Indeed, the failure to send naval forces further afield more regularly can be attributed, not just to poverty, but to a conscious strategic decision, namely the desire to have the largest possible fleet in home waters. In a way, one of the problems facing later seventeenth century governments was that their possession of a powerful new navy gave them too many attractive options, leading to the sudden changes

31

of strategy from engaging the enemy fleet, to seizing the enemy's trade, to invading the enemy's territory. The failure to evolve a more coherent 'blue water' strategy can also be attributed to a reliance on supposed historical precedents which were actually of dubious relevance in the period 1650–90, notably the notions of the self-financing war and the sovereignty of the seas.[86] On the other hand, the new opportunities presented by the navy were clearly identified in other respects. The permanent presence in the Mediterranean served the purpose of guarding English trade against depredations from the Barbary corsairs, but it also provided a permanent counterbalance to the French, Spanish, and Dutch, as shown by its reinforcement to a strength of over thirty ships in the mid-1670s when the other European states were at war, and by the plans to reinforce it further in 1678.

Above all, the mobilizations of 1668 and 1678 showed a clear recognition of the fleet's potential as a diplomatic lever: quite simply, a 'fleet in being' gave a king more flexibility in his policy-making than a fleet laid up in harbour. Moreover, the mobilizations suggest that Charles II's policy towards France might have been even more ambivalent than historians have already allowed. If Charles did take his sovereignty of the seas seriously and did accept the obvious strategic point that France could invade England more easily than could the Netherlands, then the French naval build-up in the 1660s and 1670s posed a threat to his reputation and honour which he could not ignore. It may be too strong to suggest that the French naval threat was the only issue over which Charles II seriously would have contemplated going to war with Louis XIV, but it was certainly something which Charles regarded with suspicion and alarm, and to which he reacted vigorously. The original conclusion to this paper posed a rhetorical question: just what would have happened if a French warship had refused to strike its flag to an English one in the Channel in the summer of 1678? In fact, subsequent examination of ships' journals reveals that just such an incident did occur. In July 1678, the French frigate *Perle* refused to strike to the English *Dover*, her officers claiming that if their captain did strike, 'the King would have his throat cut, meaning his head off, and that the seas were as well his master's as the King of England's'. The *Dover* closed the Frenchman on the wind, firing fifty or sixty shots at her, but the *Perle* suddenly put on sail and left the Dover wallowing in her wake. The French, unlike the Dutch, were very good at not giving Charles II the pretext to start a war.[87]

ACKNOWLEDGEMENTS

I am grateful to the earl of Dartmouth for granting permission to consult and cite his papers at the Staffordshire Record Office; to the Master and Fellows of Magdalene College, Cambridge, for granting permission to use the Pepys papers; and to Roger Morriss and Chrissie MacLeod of the National Maritime Museum for drawing my attention to the Clifford naval papers. Thanks are also due to the participants in the 1990 Dartington conference, and to the members of the seminar chaired by John Miller, Ian Roy and Henry Roseveare at the Institute of Historical Research, whose comments led to several changes being made to the paper. Above all, special thanks go to Peter Le Fevre and Sari Hornstein for their invaluable comments and advice.

NOTES

1. P.M. Kennedy, *The Rise and Fall of British Naval Mastery* (1976); D.A. Baugh,' Great Britain's "Blue Water" Policy, 1689–1815', *International History Review*, 10 (1988), 33–58; J. Hattendorf, *England in the War of the Spanish Succession: A Study in the English View and Conduct of Grand Strategy 1701–13* (New York, 1987); J.R. Jones, 'Limitations of British Sea Power in the French Wars, 1689–1815', in J. Black and P. Woodfine, eds, *The British Navy and the use of Naval Power in the Eighteenth Century* (Leicester, 1988); J. Black, 'The British Navy and British Foreign Policy in the first half of the Eighteenth Century', in J. Black and K. Schweitzer, eds, *Essays in European History in Honour of Ragnhild Hatton* (1985), 137–55.
2. P.M. Kennedy, 'The Influence and Limitations of Sea Power', *International History Review*, 10 (1988), 6–7.
3. See B.S. Capp, *Cromwell's Navy: The Fleet and the English Revolution, 1648–60* (Oxford, 1989), 73, 86–7; Black, 'Navy and British Foreign policy', 137–9.
4. Baugh, 'Blue Water Policy', *passim.*
5. J. Black, *'Natural and Necessary Enemies': Anglo-French Relations in the Eighteenth Century* (1986), *passim.*
6. Capp, *Cromwell's Navy*, 4–5, 52–3; M. Duffy, 'The Foundations of British Naval Power', in M. Duffy, ed., *The Military Revolution and the State 1500–1800* (Exeter, 1980), 52.
7. Capp, *Cromwell's Navy*, 6–9; B. Lavery, 'The Revolution in Naval Tactics 1588–1653', in M. Acerra, J. Merino & J. Meyer, eds, *Les marines de guerre Europeennes xvii–xviii siecles* (Paris, 1985), 167–74.
8. Capp, *Cromwell's Navy*, 60–114.
9. Ibid., 86–100; H. Richmond, *The Navy as an Instrument of Policy 1558–1727* (Cambridge, 1953), 127–30. The papers of Sir Thomas Clifford contain an interesting set of notes, dated Oct. and Nov. 1655, on possible naval strategies to be pursued in Cromwell's Spanish war: N[ational]

M[aritime] M[useum], MS 87/049 (provisional classification), piece nos.21–6.
10. F. Fox, *Great Ships: The Battlefleet of King Charles II* (1980), *passim.*
11. Duffy, 'Foundations of Naval Power', 53–5. Cf. Hattendorf, *War of the Spanish Succession*, 140.
12. Ibid., 1, 209–19.
13. P[ublic] R[ecord] O[fffice], S[tate] P[apers] 104/176, 177, *passim.* Longleat House, Coventry MS. 95, fos. 60–5, 75–9; Edward Hyde, earl of Clarendon, *The Life of Edward Earl of Clarendon...in which is included a Continuation of his History of the Grand Rebellion* (Oxford, 1827 edn), ii. 354–5; R.C. Anderson, ed., *The Journals of Sir Thomas Allin* (N[avy] R[ecords] S[ociety], vols 79, 80, 1939–40), i. 264, 273; R. C. Anderson, ed., *Journals and Narratives of the Third Dutch War* (NRS, vol. 86, 1946) 152, 299, 324; R. Hutton, *Charles II, King of England, Scotland, and Ireland* (Oxford, 1989), 287–8.
14. Bodleian Library, Oxford, Rawlinson MS. A.195, fo. 9; J.D. Davies, *Gentlemen and Tarpaulins: The Officers and Men of the Restoration Navy* (Oxford, 1991),134, 139,163–4, 169–70.
15. A. Grey, *Debates of the House of Commons from the Year 1667 to the Year 1694* (1763), ii. 259–63.
16. Bodleian Library, Carte MS. 40, fo. 108; Carte MS. 217, fo. 37;Folger Shakespeare Library, Washington, Newdigate newsletters 1398, 1413, 1414, 1416, 1418, 1445; H[istorical] M[anuscripts] C[ommission], *Seventh Report*, 347, 365.
17. E.g. Kennedy, *British Naval Mastery*, 47–8, and the forthcoming Harvard University Ph.D. thesis of S. Pincus. For the 'commercial' interpretation, see above all C. Wilson, *Profit and Power* (1957).
18. Richmond, *Navy as an Instrument of Policy*, 102, 149.
19. Ibid., 98.
20. B[ritish] L[ibrary], Egerton MS. 2539. fo. 112v.
21. Coventry MS. 95, fo. 60 (cf. ibid., fo. 79); Richmond, *Navy as an Instrument of Policy*, 114, 147; J.S. Corbett, *England in the Mediterranean, 1603–1713* (1904), ii. 346–7.
22. PRO, ADM[iralty papers], 3/275, pp. 56–8, 78, 80–1; SP 104/177, fos. 87v, 88v–9.
23. Richmond, *Navy as an Instrument of Policy*, 110–711, 114, 115–16, 147, 160, 189. Cf. Bod. Lib., Carte MS. 35, fos. 337, 522; BL, Harleian MS. 6845, fo. 163. On the importance of the battle of Dungeness, see Capp, *Cromwell's Navy*, 79–80.
24. R. Latham & W. Matthews, (eds.), *The Diary of Samuel Pepys* (11 vols, 1970–83), V. 35; PRO, SP 104/177, fo. 103v.
25. On the place of their merchant convoys in Dutch naval strategy, see J.R. Jones, 'The Dutch Navy and National Survival in the Seventeenth Century', *International History Review*, 10 (1988), 24–32.
26. R.0. Anderson, ed., *The Journal of the First Earl of Sandwich* (NRS, vol. 64, 1928), 180–1, 194, 199–200, 205–7, 236–54; Bod. Lib., Rawlinson MS. A.468, fos. 1–3; PRO, ADM 2/1745, fos. 122, 123, 125, 126v–7; Richmond, *Navy as an Instrument of Policy*, 149–51, 154–5.

27. PRO, SP 104/177, fos. 29, 59–60, 68, 71v, 76, 79; NMM, MS 87/049, folio 2 *passim*; Anderson, *Journals and Narratives*, 23–4, 159–60.
28. Capp, *Cromwell's Navy*, 85–100.
29. Magdalene College, Cambridge, Pepys MS. 2581, p. 213; Bod. Lib., Rawlinson MS. A.195, fo. 68; Carte MS. 34, fo. 553; NMM, MS 87/049, piece no. 28; D. Ellison, 'Lend me a Frigate', *The Mariner's Mirror*, 68 (1982), 81–2.
30. HMC, *Portland MSS.*, ii. 103; PRO, ADM 2/1745, fos. 126v–7.
31. Ibid., fo. 128.
32. PRO, SP 104/176, fos. 366–7; SP 104/177, fos. 29, 60v, 68, 76; Anderson, *Journals and Narratives*, 22–3, 159–60. Cf. Richmond, *Navy as an Instrument of Policy*, 177, for the continuation of this debate in 1673.
33. NMM, AGC/C/2 (originals of instructions to Prince Rupert, 1673). Cf. NMM, MS 87/049, piece no. 25 – seven letters of the duke of York to Clifford from June to Aug. 1672, dealing with the strategic dilemma which he faced.
34. NMM, AGC/C/2; SP 104/177, fos. 60, 62, 64–5, 68, 79, 152v–3, 162.
35. Anderson, *Sandwich Journal*, 181; PRO, ADM 2/1745, fo. 128. One commentator argued that defeating the Dutch, making them pay the costs of the war, and increasing English trade as a result would 'draw all the princes and states of the world that know the name of the English to love or dread the crowne of England': NMM, MS 87/049, piece no.28.
36. Berkeley: *Pepys's Diary*, vi. 129; J.R. Powell & E.K. Timings, eds, *The Rupert and Monck Letterbook 1666* (NRS, vol. 112, 1969), 238. Cf. the earl of Sandwich's comments in 1672 regarding his 'reputation': E.S. de Beer, ed., *The Diary of John Evelyn* (Oxford, 1955), iii. 617. On duels and quarrels in the officer corps, see Davies, *Gentlemen and Tarpaulins*, 63, 145, 147, 163–5, 171–2.
37. Anderson, *Journals and Narratives*, 47–52, 330, 382.
38. Unless otherwise stated, this and the next paragraph is based on T.W. Fulton, *The Sovereigny of the Seas* (Edinburgh, 1911), especially chs. 6–13.
39. PRO, ADM 2/1725, fos. 107v–8.
40. Fulton, *Sovereignty*, 382; Magdalene, Pepys MS. 2877, pp. 199–234.
41. BL, Sloane MS. 2439, fos. 21, 31.
42. J.R. Tanner, ed., *A Descriptive Catalogue of the Naval Manuscripts in the Pepysian Library at Magdalene College, Cambridge*, iv (NRS, vol. 57, 1922), 268, 278–9, 282–3; Lincolnshire Archives Office, Jarvis MSS. IX/1/A/4 *Anne Yacht* journal, 14 Feb. 1676.
43. Fulton, *Sovereignty*, 397–403, 432–6, 464–73, 476–82, 498–511.
44. *Pepys's Diary*, ii. 222–3; Pepys MS. 2877, *passim.*; Fulton, *Sovereignty*, 471–2, 477–8.
45. Pepys MS. 2581, p. 219.
46. Pepys MS. 2877, pp. 2–115; Fulton, *Sovereignty*, 523–6.
47. Bod. Lib., Rawlinson MS. D.147, fo. 67 & *passim*; Fulton, *Sovereignty*, 513–15.
48. Corbett, *England in the Mediterranean*, ii. 311; S. Hornstein, *The Restoration Navy and English Trade, 1654–1688* (Aldershot, 1991),155–6.

49. E.g. G.C. Gibbs, 'The Revolution in Foreign Policy', in G. Holmes, ed., *Britain after the Glorious Revolution 1689–1714* (1969), 60; J.L. Price, 'Restoration England and Europe', in J.R. Jones, ed., *The Restored Monarchy 1660–88*(1979), 128–35; Hutton, *Charles II*, 289 & *passim*.
50. *Pepys's Diary*, ix. 397. For the scale of the French build-up relative to that of England, see J. Glete, 'De Statliga Örlogsflottornas Expansion. Kapprustningen till Sjöss i Väst-och Nordeuropa 1650–80', *Studier i Aldre Historia Tillagnade Herman Shuck 5.4.1985* (Stockholm, 1985), 264, 266; Fox, *Great Ships*, 121–9.
51. M. Oppenheim, ed., *The Naval Tracts of Sir William Monson*, v (NRS, vol. 47, 1914), 16–21, 34–5; *Pepys's Diary*, ix. 447, 524; J.R. Tanner, ed., *Samuel Pepys's Naval Minutes* (NRS, vol. 60, 1925), 44, 128, 204–5, 314–15, 419–20.
52. Bod. Lib., Carte MS. 35, fos. 161v, 232, 238; Carte MS. 46, fos. 298, 306, 310–11 & *passim*; Carte MS. 47, fo. 472; All Souls College, Oxford, MS. 256, fo. 144; *Pepys's Diary*, vii. 185–6, 286–7; ibid., viii. 1, 38, 248–9, 265, 277, 602.
53. Powell & Timings, *Rupert and Monck*, 185–257.
54. Anderson, *Allin Journals*, i. 289–92; Powell & Timings, *Rupert and Monck*, 154–62. Cf. Corbett, *England in the Mediterranean*, ii. 343–4, for the seriousness with which Colbert regarded the English naval threat.
55. For a brief, accurate summary of events in the West Indies, see D. Ogg, *England in the Reign of Charles II* (Oxford, 1956), i. 307–8. During these operations, the English lost the fifth rates *Coventry* and *Colchester*.
56. R.W. Unger, 'Design and Construction of European Warships in the Seventeenth and Eighteenth Centuries', *Les marines de guerre*, 29; Fox, *Great Ships*, 139–41. For an early contemporary recognition of the qualities of French ships, see BL, Add[itional] MS. 32,094, fo. 17 (William Coventry to the duke of York, 24 Apr. 1664).
57. Coventry MS. 99, fos. 260–1.
58. Hutton, *Charles II*, 257.
59. BL, Add.MS. 32,094, fos. 212–13. Cf. PRO, ADM 2/1746, fos. 1–6.
60. Anderson, *Allin Journals*, ii, 17–24; *Pepys's Diary*, ix, 7, 18, 30, 180–1.
61. Anderson, *Allin Journals*, ii, 226; *Calendar of State Papers, Domestic Series, 1667–8*, 286, 293, 302, 310, 320, 337.
62. Hutton, *Charles II*, 264; PRO, SP 104/177.
63. H.T. Colenbrander, ed., *Bescheiden uit Vreemde Archieven Omtrent de Groote Nederlandsche-Zeeoorlogen 1652–76* (The Hague, 1919), ii. 126.
64. PRO, E/M/21/58 (typescript continuation of the *Calender of State Papers, Venetian*, for 1676–8), no. 64, Sarotti to Doge and Senate, 3 July 1676; Fulton, *Sovereignty*, 512. Cf. A.Browning, *Thomas Osborne, Earl of Danby and Duke of Leeds 1632–1712* (Glasgow, 1951), 67–8.
65. Grey, *Debates*, iv. 190. Cf. *ibid.*, iii. 62, 34–40, 96–102, 162, 296, 317–20, 323–33, 354–66, 372,417; iv. 103–4, 112–30, 180–7 & *passim*. For the 'thirty ships', see Fox, *Great Ships*, ch. 8.
66. For a recent assessment which concludes that he would have gone to war, albeit reluctantly, see Hutton, *Charles II*, 346–7.
67. BL, Add.MS. 10,115, fos. 29–31; Tanner, *Catalogue*, iv. 553.

68. Pepys MS. 2266, p.165. Figures for fireships and lesser craft (supply ships, etc.).are taken from a list dated May 1678 which retains the same numbers of major warships on all stations: Pepys MS. 2854, p.183.
69. *Journals of the House of Commons*, ix. 422–38; Grey, *Debates*, v. 28, 84, 86–7, 97, 101, 105, 107 & *passim*.
70. BL, Add.MS. 10.115, fos. 53–6; *CSPD, 1677–8*, 652; *ibid. 1678*, pp.146–7.
71. Staffordshire Record Office, MS. D(W) 1778/Ii/461, rough minutes of meetings. For Dutch documentation of the debates and decisions on strategy in 1678, see Algemeen Rijksarchief, The Hague, Admiraliteitsarchieven, collectie Evertsen, no. 19 (I am grateful to Professor J. R. Bruijn of the University of Leiden for this reference, and to the staff of the Algemeen Rijksarchief for providing me with copies of these documents).
72. Tanner, *Catalogue*, iv. 564, 567–8, 572–3; Pepys MS. 2854, p.12.
73. BL, Add.MS. 10,115, fos. 239–41.
74. Pepys MS. 2854, pp.201, 203, 210, 288, 358; *CSPD, 1678* 197; Tanner, *Catalogue*, iv. 586, 595.
75. BL, Egerton MS. 840B, fo. 24. For the activities of the fleet, see Anderson, *Allin Journals*, ii. 203–10.
76. Based on PRO, ADM 8/1, fos. 104–5; *ibid.*, fos. 93–110 give monthly disposition lists for the fleet throughout 1678.
77. Bod. Lib., Tanner MS. 39, fo. 79.
78. PRO, ADM 51/611, *Monmouth* journal, 22 Nov. 1678; Pepys MS. 2856, pp. 17, 19, 27–8, 45; HMC, *Ormonde MSS.*, new series, iv. 297–8; Tanner, *Catalogue*, iv. 629, 636.
79. See e.g. J. Ehrman, *The Navy in the War of William III* (1953) 252; E.B. Powley, *The Naval Side of King William's War* (1972), 76–8; S. Gradish, 'The Establishment of British Seapower in the Mediterranean 1689–1713', *Canadian Journal of History*, x (1975), especially pp.4, 6, 7; A.N. Ryan, 'The Royal Navy and the Blockade of Brest, 1689–1805: Theory and Practice', *Les marines de guerre*, 176; J.R. Jones, 'Limitations of British Sea Power', 43–4.
80. G.N. Clark, *The Dutch Alliance and the War against French Trade, 1688–97* (1923), 37–40.
81. PRO, ADM 3/279, pp. 16, 21; *GSPD, 1689–90*, 27, 34; Gradish, 'Establishment of British Sea Power', 4. Powley's opinion that Herbert was not an important naval advisor in 1689 and would have opposed a Mediterranean strategy, is therefore difficult to sustain: Powley, *Naval Side*, 78.
82. P. Le Fevre, 'Tangier, the Navy and its Connection with the Glorious Revolution', *The Mariner's Mirror*, 73 (1987), 187–90; Davies, *Gentlemen and Tarpaulins*, ch. 10.
83. Hornstein, *Restoration Navy and English Trade*, ch.5–6.. For the use of Gibraltar in the 1680s, see Naval Historical Library (Ministry of Defence,), MS. 169, Jonathan Gauden's letterbook, *passim*.
84. My assessment of the strategic 'plan' of 1678 and 1689 is a little more charitable than that of J.R. Jones, 'Limitations of British Sea Power', 34–7.
85. East Indies expedition: PRO, SP 104/177, fos. 88v–9. Projected Baltic squadron: ADM 106/28, fos. 38–40.

86. See Jeremy Black's perceptive comments about the 'role of mythical conceptions' in the navy of the eighteenth century: Black and Woodfine, eds., *The British Navy and the Use of Naval Power in the Eighteenth Century*, 3.

87. BL, Egerton MS. 84OB, fo. 26v; Anderson, *Allin Journals*, ii. 203–5.

3

BRITISH NAVAL POWER AND INTERNATIONAL COMMITMENTS: POLITICAL AND STRATEGIC PROBLEMS, 1688–1770

Jeremy Black

The debate over the extent to which Britain could have followed what can be, albeit at the cost of some confusion, described as a 'Blue Water' policy,[1] is obviously intimately involved with the question of Britain's international commitments. In an important sense they are of greater consequence than her strategic position and the question as to how best the country could be defended, because the possibility of invasion was directly linked to these commitments. I have argued elsewhere that naval power was of only limited value in furthering Britain's aims in continental diplomacy during the years of Walpole and Pitt.[2] In this paper I wish to range more widely and, in discussing the problems that political commitments entailed, to offer an assessment of politico-naval capabilities and weaknesses.

Britain faced two related strategic problems in the period. Neither was novel, though both were made more serious by dynastic and international developments. The problems were the weakness of Britain as a military power and her vulnerability to invasion. The developments were the growth of Bourbon strength and the growing British commitment to continental diplomacy as a consequence in part of this but more markedly as a result of the accession of foreign monarchs who, it could be argued, distorted British policy to serve their own ends in so far as the notion of national interest and policy has any meaning.[3] Any stress on these points may appear misleading in light of the triumphalist note of much writing about Britain in this period with its stress on military victory and the growth of empire. However, such a stress, though pertinent at some periods, for example immediately after the Peace of

Paris in 1763 or at a time of marked Bourbon weakness in 1787–91, was generally inappropriate. Both ministers and the political nation in general were acutely concerned about the strength and intentions of other powers and of British vulnerability in face of them.

The essential military problem was not naval, but rather that Britain increasingly sought to act as a major power while possessing a peace-time army that was that of a second-rank state. Although the size of the peace-time army increased it never matched that of France or Prussia, Austria or Russia, and the contrast was very much marked in the case of field forces. In wartime the number of British troops increased, but the size of the army was still comparatively small.

In part this was a matter of demography. Britain was not a populous country, at least in comparison with Austria or France, and the possible size of her forces was further reduced from 1689 by the stress on an all-Protestant army. This removed one of the greatest sources of soldiers, Ireland, which became instead a reservoir of troops for Bourbon recruiters, so that one of the most important contributions of Ireland to eighteenth-century British foreign policy was the provision of soldiers to fight against her armies. In part this loss was balanced after 1746 when the 'pacified' Scottish Highlands became an important source of troops. However, the demographic imbalance with France persisted.

Finance was not an important constraint on manpower, as the ability to hire foreign soldiers indicated, but there was a sustained hostility to the idea of a large army. The origins of this were various, though they were essentially political, rather than being based on any analysis of Britain's military situation. The hiring of foreign units was an obvious solution and indeed British ability to follow a militarily interventionist policy was dependent on the international military economy of Europe, the willingness of foreign powers to provide troops for hire. Furthermore, foreign troops had to be used both when Britain was invaded or threatened with invasion, as in 1715, 1745 and 1756, and when she confronted rebellion in America.

If the British army was numerically weak, dependent on foreign manpower and, with the exception of Marlborough's victories in the 1700s, not conspicuously successful in Europe, the navy was strong, reliant on national resources and generally successful, so much so that inconclusive engagements, such as Toulon in 1744, let alone the humiliation of Minorca in 1756, led to spectacular episodes of enquiry and recrimination. The navy also enjoyed an established role in British strategic thought and public debate.

The international context in which strategic thought was supposed to range was, however, far from constant. It is all to easy to use the phrase 'the Second Hundred Years War' in order to avoid probing Anglo-French relations in this period, but in fact there were periods of lessened tension and, crucially, an important alliance in 1716–31.[4] The naval consequences of this alliance have received insufficient attention, but in fact it set the pattern for public assumptions about naval power as much as the previous conflict, the War of the Spanish Succession, when the French decision to concentrate military expenditure on the army and naval resources on privateering allowed the British navy to dominate western European, including, crucially, western Mediterranean waters.[5] In fact this period of naval superiority had not been without problems, including crucially in the Mediterranean where the navy could most obviously contribute to Britain's forward military and diplomatic policy, a goal pressed by her allies, Austria and Savoy-Piedmont. In October 1701 one of the Under Secretaries, John Ellis, wrote to George Stepney, the envoy in Vienna, expressing interest in the possibility of using Adriatic ports, adding:[6]

> I cannot but join with you in thinking that nothing considerable can be done in that part of the world, without a force at sea in the Mediterranean, to procure respect from the princes and inhabitants of the coast, and to set them at liberty from the apprehension and constraints they lie under from the marine power of France and Spain in conjunction.

And yet the following year the British felt obliged to resist Austrian pressure for the dispatch of naval forces to Spanish-ruled Naples, which the Austrians were seeking to conquer. They cited the need to retain naval superiority in the Channel and William Blathwayt, the Secretary-at-War, informed Stepney:[7]

> You say right of our noble fleet and number of seamen but I don't conceive how you think we can venture twelve sail alone in the Mediterranean unless it be for a sacrifice.

If the period revealed the difficulties of combining naval strategy with the exigencies of alliance politics, it also revealed the problems of naval forces operating outside that context. In August 1703 Blathwayt wrote to Stepney:[8]

> ...our attempt upon Guadaloupe under the command of Captain Codrington has been so far unsuccessful that after plundering and spoiling the greatest part of the island we were forced to retire to our own islands by the fresh succours the French had received from Martinico. This they say has been chiefly occasioned by the disagreement of the sea commander with our land general which has been the bane of all expeditions from that against Hispaniola in Cromwell's time downwards to this last instance but the influence of the Admiralty will always prevail to make it so.

41

Despite, however, the difficulties that Britain encountered in the first three decades in the rise of her naval power, it was nevertheless the case that first French naval weakness and then the Anglo-French alliance greatly helped the British position. Spain was the seat of war during the War of the Spanish Succession and, though the Spanish navy revived subsequently, the British victory off Cape Passaro in 1718 demonstrated that her navy was still able to wield effective power in the Mediterranean. An account of naval operations in the War of the Quadruple Alliance whose third edition appeared significantly in 1739, the year when war with Spain next broke out, stated that 'the war of Sicily, wherein the fleet of Great-Britain bore so illustrious a part, that the fate of the island was wholly governed by its operations, both competitors aqreeing, that the one could not have conquered, nor the other subdued without it.' Indeed, the extent to which Britain was the unchallenged leading naval power of the period was demonstrated by her most intractable problem, the difficulty of defeating Peter the Great when his navy refused to fight. Such problems in the Baltic were a far cry from the early 1690s when France had challenged Britain effectively for control of the Channel. Even so the British were confident that their navy would prevent the Russians from dominating the Baltic, and attacking Britain's allies, Denmark and Sweden, a view that was shared by other commentators, such as the Duke of Richelieu, the French envoy in Vienna.[9]

The situation abruptly changed with the collapse of the Anglo-French alliance in 1731. The immediate response was a war panic at the prospect of a French invasion on behalf of the Jacobites.[10] The longer-term consequence was a realisation that naval superiority and strategic security would require war with France, if, as seemed likely, there was no reconciliation with her. The strategic problem of the post-1731 years was laid out clearly in an interesting pamphlet of 1742 which is worth quoting at length because of its argument that without a substantial army the British position was very parlous:[11]

... with respect to other powers, particularly France, we are now obliged to lie upon the defensive, and can only hope to protect ourselves from being invaded, without any ability to attack that kingdom ... a considerable body of regular troops at hand, which alone can convince the people of France of our power to give them assistance. This is, perhaps, now the only method of breaking the strength of the French monarchy, which is abundantly fortified on its inland frontiers; and whilst it has the whole body of its people within undisturbed, will always be able to exert a prodigious force at these extremities: but an attack by sea in the heart of its most fruitful provinces, would interrupt its commerce, and suppress its revenues, and raise a spirit in their people, which they might never afterwards be able to break; but all this it is in vain to think of, without we support a sufficient land-force.

Admitting the utmost that can be attributed to our fleet alone; Allowing, though it is by no means true, that it can effectually guard our own coasts; is it not evident that our weakness at land must diminish its force? for we must always reserve our most potent squadron at hand, for our own defence against an invasion; and the remainder is all that we can employ at any distance; which, probably, may not exceed the French squadron in the Streights, or West Indies: so that our weakness at land actually deprives us of a superiority at sea. This at the same time is sure to create an ignorant clamour; and the wisdom of a minister in not leaving us unguarded at home, shall be branded for cowardice; and the squadrons that are reserved for our own defence, shall be ridiculed, and stigmatized with being pacifick ... it is thought by some projecting persons, that we ought, in the beginning of this war, to have dispatched almost all our fleet, and our experienced regiments to the West fridies. This might have been done indeed, if our regular land force was at all numerous, and would admit of any deduction for foreign service, consistent with our own domestic security. But if we had thus ventured in our present circumstances, and left this nation exposed with only eight or ten thousand disciplined soldiers, and a weak squadron, the least motion of the troops of France towards Dunkirk, Calais, or the coasts of Normandy, or Brittany, would justly have given us severe uneasiness: And the equipment of a French squadron, or an account of their collecting transports together, would have immediately thrown us into the utmost terror and confusion.

The pamphlet was correct in its arguments, and Walpole himself had in November 1739 pointed out that naval force alone would not force Spain to peace, though the author overlooked the political opposition to the idea of a larger army. Indeed, the attempt to raise the forces at George II's disposal by financing Hanoverian military activity was to cause a serious parliamentary and political storm in 1742–3. In addition, the argument that amphibious operations against continental France could make a material difference to war with France was not to be proved by experience during the Austrian Succession and Seven Years' Wars. The central point, however, was that without a large army British naval options were limited so long as the French kept a fleet in being was definitely true. At a time of Anglo-Spanish conflict and Anglo-French tension in 1740 Earl Waldegrave, the envoy in Paris, reported, 'Their preparations in the sea-ports go on. I really think they mean nothing more by them than to keep us on the watch and oblige us to increase our armaments and consequently our expenses.' The Duke of Newcastle, Secretary of State for the Southern Department, replied 'the truth is the French preparations do necessarily oblige us to keep such a fleet here as is in other respects useless and might be much more advantageously employed elsewhere.' As Walter Titley, British envoy in Copenhagen, pointed out after the battle of Toulon, 'it is not their interest to risk their moderate sea-force against the English, which is so much superior and can soon be repaired in case of ill success.' Naval strength did not preclude fears of invasion. William Hay, a Walpolean Whig, told the House of Commons in 1738, 'It may be thought, and I have often heard it said, that our fleet will protect us: but our fleet is not always sure of meeting an enemy; and if that expectation should fail what reserve have we then left but our land forces?' Nine years later Newcastle was worried about the build-up of French forces in the Channel ports, including conquered Ostend.[12] This situation put a strategic and diplomatic premium on the destruction of the French navy, lending military point to the sense of humiliation and dissatisfaction that followed failures to achieve this end. The nature of naval operations was not, however, conducive to forcing an unwilling opponent to fight in a position of inferiority.

A parallel can be drawn with the land warfare of the period which was also frequently inconclusive from the point of field engagements with, at the risk of being fanciful, further comparisons being possible between on the one hand blockades and the struggle to protect trade from privateers and on the other sieges and the attempt to control areas in order to use them for logistical purposes. Generals could generally avoid unwelcome engagements by retiring behind natural or artificial defensive features, and it was not easy to force them to fight. However, a comparison between the naval and land warfare that Britain was involved in suggests that it was more common for her to fight battles on land and that most of her victories and defeats were on that element. In part obviously this reflected the comparative numerical advantage that she enjoyed at sea, and the consequent unwillingness of her opponents to fight, but it is also clear that land operations were more conducive to engagements.

The continued existence of the French fleet and the failure in particular to destroy it in 1744, when opportunities presented themselves in the Channel and the Mediterranean, had considerable strategic consequences at the time of the '45. It increased the danger of a French landing on the south coast which was in fact erroneously reported. The ministry ordered the navy to prevent French moves in the Channel, Admiral Martin being instructed in July, when information was received that the French had decided to invade, to prevent any ships from leaving Brest. The Duke of Newcastle wrote in October 1745, 'Admiral Martin is cruising off the Lizard with a very considerable squadron. Admiral Vernon continues in the Downs; and we have a great number of small ships in different parts of the Channel.'[13] Confidence on this head was, however, limited. Horace Mann was not the only commentator who feared storms. In August Newcastle's private secretary Andrew Stone observed:

> We hope we shall soon have a pretty strong squadron in the Channel: But I know too well, the great delays and uncertaintys that service is liable to, to depend very much upon it. When Ostend is gone (as it will soon be) I tremble to think of the constant alarms we shall be subject to.

That December Stephen Weston, an Exeter cleric, complained:

> I doubt should any attempt be made from Brest or St Malo at this time we should fall a too easy prey since land forces we have none but the garrison at Plymouth, and that just now reduced by a draught for Bristol; part of our Western Squadron too being lately sailed to strengthen Vernon in the Downs, I think we are in a state to be pity'd, and the utmost to be hoped from us is to run away with the money we are raising, leaving our estates and houses to the rage of the invaders. We must pray therefore for a North East or North West wind to shut up the western ports of France, since a South East or South West brings our enemies upon us, and at the same time denys us the assistance of our friends.[14]

These fears were to be justified in part. Cumberland's pursuit of Bonnie Prince Charlie was to be constrained by the fear of an invasion of the South coast. On 12 December 1745 Newcastle wrote to him:[15]

> His Majesty having received an account from Admiral Vernon, that a considerable number of vessels, besides small boats, are assembled at Dunkirk, and that there is the greatest reason to believe that an attempt will be immediately made to land a body of troops from hence on some part of the southern or eastern coast ... your Royal Highness should immediately return to London, with the rest of the cavalry and foot, that are now with you.

Arguably the failure to defeat the Jacobites when they rashly invaded England in the face of far superior forces, was of crucial importance in the War of the Austrian Succession for it ensured that Britain would open the 1746 campaign with most of her forces at home and, thus, that the opportunity to challenge France's gains of 1745 in the Austrian Netherlands would be lost. To that extent the '45 was a considerable success for France, far more of a diversionary achievement than British attacks on the French coast.

The role of seapower in the '45 can be seen in a number of lights. The British were able to take for granted the use of the sea to move troops up the east coast and across the North Sea, thus avoiding most of the problems posed by an invasion when most of the army was abroad, and enabling British forces to operate or maintain a presence in two spheres at once. British naval power also blocked French schemes. In January 1746 the French foreign minister, the Marquis D'Argenson, wrote to the Bishop of Rennes, the envoy in Madrid, 'Nous sommes meme dans l'incertitude si le corps de 12000 hommes qui est prest à s'embarquer sur nos costes pour passer dans les Isles Britanniques, pourra suivre sa destination. Il se trouve presentement arresté par la flotte de l'amiral Vernon qui croise dans le Canal, et qu'on asseure etre composée de 30 vaisseaux de guerre.' And yet later that month George Grenville wrote from London, 'the Spanish men of war are coming with 5 large French ships from Ferrol to Brest which spreads some terror for fear of our coast.'

No crisis comparable to the '45 was ever again to occur. During subsequent French invasion attempts, as in 1759 and 1779, there was no indigenous pro-French activity and therefore the strategic situation was different. In December 1770, when war with the Bourbons over the Falklands appeared imminent, there was opposition in the Council to the idea of sending a fleet to Gibraltar and Jamaica, because it was feared that it might leave the British 'coasts exposed to be insulted', not because of the prospect of any co-operation with domestic rebellion.[16] In 1745–6 the British army was torn between two competing demands: the Jacobite army and the prospect of a French invasion. By making the latter more or less likely, the balance of naval power affected operations against the Jacobites, who were the more immediate military threat. In contrast, durinq subsequent invasion years it was possible to match British army and naval strength and deployments to a common threat.

During the rest of the War of the Austrian Succession there was an obvious divergence between growing British naval superiority and the dismal progress ot the campaigns in the Low Countries. In consequence, and in marked contrast to the situation during the War of the Spanish Succession, the hope developed that naval success could compensate for continental defeats. Theophilus Leigh, Master of Balliol, observed in July 1747, 'We have had better success by Sea than Land; I wish one might Balance the other.'[17] This, however, placed a new politico-strategic burden on the navy for it was now required to obtain trans-oceanic advantages, an obligation that necessitated the mastery of home and European waters that would permit the trans-oceanic dispatch of major naval forces. In part these ideas were of long standinq, reflectinq a traditional optimistic public assessment of naval capability but the political need for them can be traced to 1745. It was in that year that the hopes of defeating France militarily that had been so marked in 1742–3, especially after Dettingen, were replaced by the realisation that it would in fact be difficult to stop the French triumphing by land. In August 1744 Frederick the Great attacked Austria, beginning the Second Silesian War, and preventing the Austrians from maintaining their military pressure on eastern France. The following year Saxe conquered much of the Austrian Netherlands, including Ghent, Bruges, Ostend and Nieuport, a good example of the inaccuracy of the oft-repeated claim that campaigns in this period were slow and inconsequential. In 1745 the French lost Louisbourg and Cape Breton island,[18] and the proposition of an exchange for French gains in the Austrian Netherlands as part of a peace, based on the *status quo ante bellum* emerged speedily. This placed an immediate strategic burden on the navy, the defence of Cape Breton. That led to problems the following year when the French sought to regain the island. There were now heavier strategic and political burdens on the British admirals entrusted with keeping the French fleet in its harbours or defeating it if it sailed out. In June 1746 Stephen Weston wrote to his brother from Exeter:

> We are very much troubled by the news we have had several days of the French fleet having slipped Martin, and fear we must expect some severe blow in some sensible part or other; Cape Breton, Jamaica, Minorca, and Ireland are all guessed at.

Newcastle complained more pointedly to Cumberland:

> The only contretems we have had, was Admiral Martin's ignorance or what is worse, letting the French fleet get clear of him. Should they go to North America, and make conquests there; We shall lose both the means of making peace, or war. For when once they have either retaken Cape Breton; or taken Newfoundland, or Nova Scotia (which will be the equivalent for it) we have no longer in our hands the means of purchasing peace of France; or of inducing this Nation to carry on the war.[19]

Anville's squadron was wrecked, fortunately for the British, for it is far from clear what the consequences of the loss of Cape Breton would have been; while the following May Anson defeated La Jonquière off Cape Finistere and on 14 October 1747 Hawke won the most brilliant action of the war, the Second Battle of Cape Finisterre, leaving Newcastle to write to Cumberland, 'All difficulties that could be apprehended in Parliament will by this be removed, the pride of France a little humbled, and I hope our allies so far encouraged, that your Royal Highness will find them willing, and able to exert themselves for their own safety and support.' Newcastle was correct to point to the parliamentary consequences of victory. On the same day Lady Elizabeth Yorke,

Lord Chancellor Hardwicke's daughter, who was shortly to marry Anson, wrote to her sister-in-law Marchioness Grey, pointing out the military advantages of the victory and adding, 'Admiral Hawke has likewise disappointed the designs of more than the French, it having been intended by the opposition to begin their attack this session by falling upon the Admiralty; now it is thought that this scheme must be defeated, since after the late repeated successes, such an attempt cannot be very popular or successful.' Seven years earlier, the situation had been very different for Sir Robert Walpole, Lady Cecilia Finch writing 'the seasons so far advanced that it is almost impossible to flatter one self anything considerable can be performed time enough to open the Parliament with a speech giving an account of the success of our arms abroad which would silence the babblers at once by leaving no room to inveigh against the conduct of the present administration which their zeal and malice will prompt them to blame without making any allowance for the bad winds.'[20]

Victory had therefore transformed the invasion threats of 1744–5 and the danger of the loss of Cape Breton in 1746 into a completely different political, strategic and diplomatic situation. The angry debates over naval policy that had characterised the earlier years of the war had ended, so that Sandwich could write in November 1747, 'it is plain that our fleet has honour and great support.'[21] The navy ended the war in a rich glow of success, at the same time as the disadvantages of alliance politics and a continental military commitment were abundantly brought home by the collapse of the Dutch frontier, with the French capture of Bergen-op-Zoom in 1747 and Maastricht the following year, and the Dutch pressure for peace. Newcastle wrote after another naval success in early 1748, 'though we have our mortifications, the enemy have theirs also. Their trade is absolutely ruined for the present, and bankrupts swarm in all the great French towns.'[22]

And yet over the next few years British foreign policy was to be dominated by an interventionist diplomacy, that placed little weight on naval power, and entailed commitments to continental affairs greater than any peacetime diplomacy since the reign of George I and the first years of that of George II. The consequences of this policy for naval affairs are open to discussion. It could be suggested that the deterioration in Franco-Spanish relations that led to the Austro-Spanish Treaty of Aranjuez of 14 June 1752 was the single most important factor behind British naval success in the Seven Years War. Spain remained neutral until 1762 and thus the arithmetic of naval confrontation that had in the previous war limited British flexibility was vitally altered, a change that helps to explain Vergennes' determination to gain Spanish assistance in the War of American Independence. However, important as this development was, it cannot really be ascribed to Britain, though the government sought to further both the settlement of the Italian question and the rift between France and Spain. The British ministry had offered naval assistance to the new Austro-Spanish alignment, the Earl of Holdernesse, Secretary of State for the Southern Department, writing to the Earl of Rochford, envoy in Turin, 'The very notion of His Majesty's supporting this great alliance, with his maritime force, gives the greatest weight and sanction to it.'[23] This was not in fact the case.

Although the British contributed to the new alignment in the western Mediterranean, the bulk of their diplomatic attention in 1749–53 was devoted to attempts to improve the so-called Old Alliance with Austria and the United Provinces and, in particular, to the Imperial Election Scheme. This represented a classic instance of preparing to fight the last war. Because the Imperial Succession had helped undermine Austrian strength in the early 1740s, the issue was to be settled. Because the defence of the Low Countries had been inhibited during the same conflict by Austrian and Dutch weaknesses and commitments, in British eyes that tended to forget the '45, both powers were to be strengthened, especially by settling disputes over the Austrian Netherlands and by creating an alliance system that would comprise most ot the German states and restrain Prussian aggression.

Naval power was essentially immaterial to this diplomatic strategy, especially because Austrian defensive and offensive interests in Italy, which had played such a major role in Anglo-Austrian relations in the 1700s and 1710s and during the periods of effective alliance between 1731 and 1733 and 1742 and 1748, had been settled by the reconciliation with Spain. The British government believed that the strength of the fleet influenced the continental powers. In October 1753 Newcastle, since 1748 Secretary of State for the Northern Department, wrote to Robert Keith, the envoy at Vienna, 'His Majesty's fleet, (though at a very great expence), is in a better condition, than it ever was known to be, in time of peace: and the great effect, which the superiority of the King's navy, the last war, had towards obtaining the peace; shows how necessary and effectual, the keeping up that fleet, may be for the preservation of it.' Keith dutifully replied that the Austrian Chancellor, Count Kaunitz 'was very glad to hear, that the King's Royal Navy is in such a condition, as to promise us a superiority at sea in all events. He knows of what consequence our naval force is; how much it contributed to our obtaining the last peace; and how necessary, and essential, the keeping up our fleet is for the preservation of it.'[24]

In practice, however, the powers of central and eastern Europe were less impressed by or interested in British naval power and indeed a failure to consider the views of other powers adequately has weakened some discussion of British naval capability.[25] There is obviously evidence of particular episodes in which British naval power featured as a possible factor. In July 1748 the French foreign minister Puysieulx warned the Marshal-Duke of Richelieu, who was to conquer Minorca in 1756, that if he was to form a plan of operations for an Italian war he must anticipate 'que le passage par la Mediterranée, s'il ne nous est pas ferme, nous sera du moins fort contesté.' The following month Frederick II wrote to his sister, the Princess Royal of Sweden, asking what help France could provide her Swedish ally in her confrontation with Russia, which was allied with Austria and Britain, 'Comment une escadre française pourrait-elle traverser la Manche, dès que l'Angleterre et la Hollande ne voudraient pas lui en donner le passage?' The following year Sir Charles Hanbury-Williams, the British envoy in Dresden, noted the suggestion of an Austrian minister that Russia should ask the British to send a fleet to the Baltic if Marshal Saxe pursued his plans to acquire Courland.[26]

Naval power was clearly important in the Baltic and this had allowed Britain to play a role in Baltic diplomacy in, for example, the Dano-Swedish conflict in 1700, the last years of the Great Northern War and 1726–7. In 1747 the Russians had pressed for naval assistance against Sweden, Lord Hyndford reporting from St Petersburg that Czarina Elizabeth thought 'that His Majesty seemed to expect too much of her, in that she should, without any assistance of money or troops begin the war against Sweden alone, upon bare appearance; but that, if His Majesty would enter into a treaty for that purpose, and send a squadron of ships into the Baltic, she would attack Sweden on the side of Finland.' In an interesting reference to the possibility of using naval action against privateers to cover a political commitment, as had indeed happened in the Great Northern War against Sweden, Hyndford continued, 'His Majesty had a very good pretext of sending a squadron into that sea, as she was positively informed, that there would be a number of French privateers sent thither as soon as the season was open, to disturb the English navigation and trade with this Empire.' Hyndford later wrote, 'I believe this court has so great a mind to drive the successor and all his French adherents out of Sweden, that, if the king could spare but five or six ships of war for the Baltic to sustain the Russians, the Empress would undertake the thing of herself.'[27]

However, the limitations of British naval power as a diplomatic tool in the Baltic had been exposed in 1720 and were to be again in 1791, and it is difficult to believe that Russia did not attack Sweden in 1747 because Britain would not supply a few warships. In the case of the Empire, which became the focus of diplomatic activity and speculation in 1750 after the ending of the Baltic crisis, British naval power was of little value. In 1753 the Prussian envoy in Paris, the Jacobite Lord Marshal of Scotland, pointed out to Frederick II that he had no reason to fear a British maritime war and he referred to the vulnerability of the Electorate of Hanover,[28] the central question mark against British diplomatic and military plans. In their German diplomacy the British relied on financial inducements and talk of shared interests. Militarily they reterred to the support of Austria and Russia. There was no role for naval power comparable, for example, to its importance in sustaining Anglo-Piedmontese co-operation for much of the first half of the century.[29]

Nevertheless, though there was the usual post-war military demobilization, one that was aided by the relatively more peaceful post-war atmosphere, in contrast to the situation after the Nine Years and Spanish Succession wars, ministers remained convinced of the importance of naval power. They found themselves, however, accused of failing to take adequate steps to counter Bourbon colonial and naval moves. The opposition used this as evidence of a supposed failure to protect national interests, complementing criticism of an excessive concern for continental diplomacy and serving to illustrate the supposed failure to define national interests correctly that the latter was supposed to indicate. In 1748 the *Craftsman*, an opposition newspaper, claimed 'The French see our superiority at sea, and are providing against it; therefore our countrymen should think what proper instructions to give their representatives on that account.' The following spring another such paper, the *Westminster Journal* urged the need to defend Britain's rights in North America firmly, 'We need not fear the consequence of such strictness, while we have a fleet capable to vindicate the justice of our conduct.' The *Remembrancer* claimed, 'we have exhausted ourselves compleatly, in a cause, that of all the powers of Europe, we were the last, and least, concerned in: The balance of power at land was the bubble we fought for; whereas the commerce and navigation of the World, and the sovereignty of the Ocean, ought to have been the principal objects of their attention.' Another London newspaper, *Old England*, stated that France 'will not be forward to show that resentment further than in words, it they see us forward to vindicate our claim in the way of our natural strength, by a maritime force, without engaging in fruitless and expensive alliances on the Continent.'[30]

Such language was also used in opposition political circles, Admiral Vernon writing in 1749 to Sir Francis Dashwood, a fellow MP:

I look on the fate of this country to be drawing to a speedy period whenever France shall attain to a superior maritime power to Britain, which by the present of Cape Breton, we have given them an extensive foundation for ... I may say without the spirit of prophecy, that whenever they think

51

themselves so, the first blow they will strike, will be to strip us, of every one of our sugar colonies, which I know to be easily attainable by them, whenever they have a superior force by sea; and that the natural consequence of that will be, that you will by the same blow, lose all your American colonies as to their dependence on Britain.

And then what must become of a nation ... with eighty millions of debt, and deprived of those branches of commerce that principally produced the revenues, to pay the interest of those debts, is a melancholy consideration.

The same month Puysieulx wrote to the French chargé d'affaires in London that he saw by the proceedings of Parliament, 'que le sentiment de la nation seroit de prendre moins de part dans les affaires de terre et beaucoup plus dans celles de mer et de commerce.' The French remained convinced of this theme. François de Bussy, formerly envoy in London and the ambivalent British agent 101, in a memorandum of 1751 wrote:

Les Anglais ont une mesure pour les affaires de mer très differente de celles des autres nations, leur superiorité dans cette partie les ebloüit au plint que tout ce qui est usurpation de leur part leur semble juste et dans cette persuasion toute querelle, toute depense de mer est soutenüe par eux sans aucune difficulté, et nulle part les ordres de la cour d'Angleterre ne sont plus mal executés que sur la mer et dans le colonies angloises. Tous les ecrits publies a Londres ne respirent que le dessein de s'emparer des colonies francois et l'on y met serieusement en principe que la seule ressource de l'Angleterre pour payer ses dettes est de ruiner le commerce de France.

Later that year Mirepoix, the ambassador in London, commented on the support for naval war against France, adding that the government realised that it was impossible to keep any war with France simply naval 'mais les ministres ne sont point assés accredités pour dissuader le public, ni asses fermes pour resister a ses impulsions.'[31]

The ministry kept a close eye on French naval developments, and they were indeed the prime target of British intelligence.[32] However, though French naval power revived there was a certain amount of confidence in British ministerial circles, not least because of Bourbon disunity. In 1753 Joseph Yorke, the envoy at The Hague, doubted that France would fight to support Frederick II, 'Spain is not disposed to act with them, and they are too sensible of the weight of England by sea, to risk their marine before it is recovered.' However, at the same time there was an awareness that British naval power might not be equal to all the demands that might be placed upon it. Newcastle wrote to Yorke that summer about the negotiations between the British and French East India Companies:

You may assure The Princess Royal, that the King will not suffer anything to be done, that may tend to secure France, in case of war, against the superiority of His Majesty's fleet, in any part of the world ... Our Directors think that a neutrality, confined to the other side of The Cape, would be found more advantageous to us than to France; As the French East India ships, in the Indies, could easily be turned into ships of force; which ours could not; and we should, by that means, be obliged to have a constant squadron there, in time of war, which would lessen our naval strength in other parts.[33]

Despite this concern about possible naval deployment, it would be fair to say that the ministry was more worried in 1753 by the defence of Hanover against possible Prussian attack. This concern dictated alliance politics, and British policy in this period justified the response the Earl of Rochford had given to a Sardinian minister in 1749 who 'had heard we were going to put our naval force upon a better foot than ever, and that we intended for the future to place our chief strength in it,' to which Rochford had replied that the government thought that it could only preserve the balance of power in cooperation with allies. The same year Newcastle argued that France would outdo Britain in any maritime struggle unless Britain had continental allies to divert her strength.[34] Indeed the response of the ministry to the worsening of relations with France over North America in 1754–5 was a determination to strengthen Britain's continental alliances. Far from there being any notion that maritime strength could bring conquests that would compensate for continental vulnerability, the ministry based its diplomacy on the defence of Hanover. Bussy had written in 1751, '... du coté de la mer ... l'Angleterre n'a point d'alliés a consulter, ses conseils et ses operations dans cette partie ne dependent qu d'elle même', but the ministry did not seek this simplicity.[35]

That Britain ended up fighting with only one significant ally, Prussia, and without the support of her former partners in the old Alliance was in part fortuitous, though attempts have been made to argue that it was an inevitable consequence of changes in the European system.[36] However this diplomatic failure paradoxically helped to free the question of naval strategy from diplomatic entanglements. There was pressure for the commitment of naval forces to the Baltic, a point pressed hard by Frederick II who anticipated that it would help him with Russia and Sweden. This demand was supported by the Duke of Cumberland who in 1757 commanded the forces defending Hanover and was convinced of the need to please Frederick. In May 1757 he wrote to the Earl of Holdernesse, the Secretary of State for the Northern Department:

I am sorry to say that, though the dispositions which you have acquainted me are made for the sea operations this year, I see but little hopes of a squadron co-operating with the King of Prussia in the Baltic this year. Had the measure been thought proper, which I can not help thinking still, might have been, as I see three great such fleets sent to sea (viz the western squadron, that of the Mediterranean, as well as Holburn's, reinforced, to North America) which, according to the best account sent from France, will, nowhere meet with any kind ot opposition from their naval force; a very small diminution from those three great fleets, would have formed such a squadron, as might, and would in all probability, have restored His Majesty's weight in the *North*, where it is but too apparent, that the scale of France, at present preponderates.

The following month he returned to the theme:

I regret either our not being able or not sending a fleet into the Baltic, which would certainly not only have greatly pleased the King of Prussia, but would have greatly restored the weight His Majesty naturally ought to have in the North.

However, Holdernesse had already explained that diplomatic obligations had to take second place to naval priorities:

The utility of sending a strong squadron to the Baltic becomes every day more apparent; but I cannot pretend to say there is any great prospect that such an additional number of men, as this service would require, are to be found; though if we may credit some fresh advices from Toulon, there are but eight ships of the line in that harbour fit for the sea, since the departure of the four, supposed to be gone to America; in which case the force destined for the Mediterranean might be diminished, and other objects in part answered by it.[37]

This was a long way from the Wars of the Spanish and Austrian Successions and the War of the Quadruple Alliance when the navy had had an important politico-strategic commitment, namely the control of the Western Mediterranean in order to further the plans of allies in Italy and, in the case of the War of the Spanish Succession, Spain. The absence of any such commitment during the Seven Years' War helped to release British naval power to concentrate on the challenge of France, though it would of course be misleading to suggest that politics played no part in the deployment of naval power. The policy of raids on the French coast was essentially political in its origin.[38] Pitt could see such raids as affecting French troop deployments, though the 4th Duke ot Bedford was more dubious, writing in July 1761 to George II's favourite, the Earl of Bute:

Mr. Pitt tells you, that by the conquest of Belleisle, you are enabled to spread the alarm so thoroughly over the whole coast of France, which is on the Ocean, that the People won't be able to sleep quietly in their beds. But can we do more? Upon the continent of France, after they have had so long a time to guard against us in the material places, such as Bordeaux, Rochefort, Brest, L'Orient and St. Malo, I fear not, especially as it will be impossible to spare any more troops from hence or Ireland, without leaving your own coasts liable to be insulted, even by a handful of men. What then in our situation can be expected from our efforts during this summer from Belleisle? Why possibly the taking another island, or burning a few miserable villages on the Continent.

Bedford continued by doubting that Martinique would fall if the war continued, a view that was to be proved inaccurate, before arguing that it would be impossible to

...induce the French to relinquish a right of fishery, which if they do, must put a final blow to their being any longer a naval power, though possessing a coast in the Channel and the ocean ... Indeed the endeavouring to drive France entirely out of any naval power, is fighting against Nature, and can tend to no one good to this country, but on the contrary must excite all the naval powers in Europe to enter into a confederacy against us, as adopting a system, viz: that of a monopoly of all naval power, which would be at least as dangerous to the liberties of Europe, as that of Louis the 14th was.[39]

The striking feature of this debate, however, was that it was conducted in terms of what Britain could achieve through the use of naval power against France. The continental dimension was almost entirely absent. Whereas in the 1720s statesmen had discussed whether British naval power could affect actions by Austria and Russia that essentially owed nothing to maritime considerations, during the Seven Years' War the central question was one of the direct impact of naval power. Instead of discussing whether the bombardment of Naples or Riga might influence policy, it was possible to discuss the actual implications of seizing particular French colonies.

It was not surprising that this shift encouraged a more optimistic assessment of the navy. It was not simply that the navy and amphibious operations were more successful in the Seven Years' War than in the previous conflict, but also that their activities and triumphs could be seen clearly as designed to further British objectives. The assessment of national interests is always controversial, but it was easier to assert it at a time when military actions were clearly related to views of such interests. The contrast between the popularity of naval operations off Canada and operations in Mediterranean waters during the War of the Austrian Succession was clear, and, again, it was not only relative success that played a role. In the Seven Years' War it was the European operations, especially when unsuccessful or only partially successful, that enjoyed limited popularity. In contrast, colonial operations were on the whole seen as obviously serving national interests. An important reason was that in these operations Britain did not need to consult the views of allies. She had last had to do so in the colonial sphere in the wars of the Spanish Succession and Quadruple Alliance, but thereafter the damaging accusations of surrender to the views of allies or the Hanoverian interests of the monarch that so often compromised the public reputation of European operations were absent. Given the importance of political support in British naval activity, this factor was of some significance though it is difficult to assess how far specific naval decisions should be traced to the political context.

This paper has therefore sketched a shift of naval commitment that it is argued reflected diplomatic and strategic exigencies and in turn affected the political context that helped to shape expectations concerning naval power. Put simply, the move away from Europe,[40] helped to create a different political context for the use of naval power that altered the politico-naval capabilities and weaknesses of the Royal Navy. The navy had always been helped in its public and political reputation by the fact that it needed the support of allies relatively little for its operations, in marked contrast to the army. The growing weakness of Dutch naval power[41] furthered this process. From the Seven Years' War on this trend was complete, and naval action could be envisaged simply in an Anglo-Bourbon context, as in the plans to support colonial pretensions after the Seven Years' War.[42] The navy could be seen as truly British, not only in its composition but in its objectives. If the possible use of naval power would have been no more able to prevent the First Partition of Poland (1772) or to intimidate Russia during the Ochakov crisis (1791) than it had been able to persuade Peter the Great to restore some of his conquests from Sweden, the navy could nevertheless be seen clearly as a force designed and commonly used to support what were generally seen as the national goals: the security of Britain and her colonies, and maritime hegemony.

ACKNOWLEDGMENTS

I am grateful for the support of the British Academy, the Wolfson Foundation and the Staff Travel and Research Fund of Durham University.

NOTES

1. D. Baugh, 'Great Britain's "Blue Water" Policy, 1689–1815', *International History Review*, 10 (1988), 33–58.
2. J.M. Black, 'The British Navy and British Foreiqn Policy in the First Half of the Eighteenth Century', in Black and K.W. Schweizer, eds, *Studies in European History in honour of Ragnhild Hatton* (Lennoxville, Quebec, 1985), 137–55; Black, 'Naval power and British foreign policy in the age of Pitt the Elder', in Black and P. Woodfine, eds, *The British Navy and the Use of Naval Power in the Eighteenth Century* (Leicester, 1988), 91–107.
3. J.M. Black, *British Foreign Policy in the Age of Walpole* (Edinburgh, 1985), 27–48; Black, 'The Tory View of Eighteenth-Century British Foreign Policy', *Trivium*, 23 (1988), 127–48; Black, 'The Revolution and the Development of English Foreign Policy', in E. Cruickshanks, ed., *By Force or By Default? The Revolution of 1688* (Edinburgh, 1989), 135–58.
4. J.M. Black, *Natural and Necessary Enemies. Anglo-French Relations in the Eighteenth Century* (1986)
5. A valuable recent account of these years is provided by John Hattendorf, *England in the War of the Spanish Succession. A Study of the English View and Conduct of Grand Strategy, 1702–1712* (New York, 1987).
6. B[ritish] L[ibrary], Add. MS 7074 f.49, Ellis to Stepney, 17 October 1701.
7. New Haven, Beinecke Library, Osborn Shelves (hereafter Beinecke, Osborn), Blathwayt to Stepney, 28 February 1702; Maidstone, Kent Archive Office, U 1590 053/10, Secretary of State James Vernon to Alexander Stanhope, envoy at The Hague.
8. Beinecke, Osborn, Blathwayt Box 21, Blathwayt to Stepney, 6 Aug. 1703.
9. Anon, *An Account of the Expedition of the British Fleet to Sicily, in the Years 1718, 1719 and 1720*, (3rd ed., London, 1739) p.88; P[ublic] R[ecord] O[ffice], S[tate] P[apers] 90/20, Du Bourgay, envoy to Berlin, to Viscount Townshend, Secretary of State for the Northern Department, 9 April, Townshend to Du Bourgay, 31 May 1726; Paris, Bibliothèque Victor Cousin, Fonds Richelieu 31 f.63, 65, Richelieu to Marquis de Silly, 25 May, St Saphorin, British envoy to Vienna, to Lord Glenorchy, envoy in Copenhagen, 1 June 1726.
10. J.M. Black and A. Reese, 'Die Panik von 1731', in J. Kunisch, ed., *Expansion und Gleichgewicht. Studien zur europäischen Mächtepolitik des ancien régime* (Berlin, 1986), 69–95; Black, *The Collapse of the Anglo-French Alliance 1727–1731* (Gloucester, 1987), 202–5.
11. Anonymous, *A Letter from a By-Stander to a Member of Parliament: Wherein is Examined what Necessity there is for the Maintenance of a Large Regular Land Force in this Island* (London, 1742) 19, 23–5.
12. W. Cobbett, *A Parliamentary History of England* (36 vols., London, 1806–20) vol.11, 190; PRO, SP 78/223 ff. 61, 111, Waldegrave to Newcastle, 8 June, Newcastle to Waldegrave, 12 June 1740; Farmington, Connecticut, Lewis Walpole Library, Weston papers vol.14, Titley to Edward Weston, 21 April 1744; Northampton, County Record Office, L (C) 1734, 3 Feb.; BL, Add. MS 32,810 f.111, Newcastle to Sandwich, 2 Oct. 1747.

13. PRO, SP 43/111, meeting of Lords Justices, 24 July 1745; Carlisle, Cumbria Record Office, D/Pen Acc. 2689, Newcastle to Viscount Lonsdale, 3 Oct. 1745.

14. W.S. Lewis, ed., *The Yale Edition of Horace Walpole's Correspondence* (New Haven, 1937–83), Mann-Walpole Correspondence III, 120, 19 Oct. 1745; Farmington, Weston papers 16, Stone to Weston, 2 Aug., Stephen to Edward Weston, 25 Dec. 1745.

15. Windsor, Royal Archives, Cumberland papers (hereafter RA. CP.) 8/9, Newcastle to Cumberland, 12 Dec. 1745.

16. Paris, Ministere des Affaires Etrangères, Correspondance Politique (hereafter AE.CP.) Espagne 488 f.48, D'Argenson to Rennes, 11 January 1746; San Marino, California, Huntington Library, Stowe Manuscripts, STG Box 191 (6), George to Thomas Grenville, 28 Jan. 1746; PRO, SP 37/7 f.260, Minutes of Council, 19 Dec. 1770; J. Black, *Culloden and the '45* (Stroud, 1990).

17. Oxford, Balliol College Library, Mss 403 f.27, Leigh to Lydia, widow of 1st Duke of Chandos, 5 July 1747.

18. M. Mimler, *Der Einfluss kolonialor Interessen in Nordamerika auf die Strategie und Diplomatie Grossbritanniens während des Osterreichischen Erbfolgekrieges 1744–1748. Ein Beitrag zur Identitatsbestimmung des britischen Empire um die Mitte des 18 Jahrhunderts* (Hildesheim, 1983), pp. 48–90.

19. Farmington, Weston Papers 18, Stephen to Edward Weston, 28 June 1746, BL, Add. MS 32,707 f.390–v, Newcastle to Cumberland 3 July 1746.

20. RA.CP. 29/145 Newcastle to Cumberland, 27 Oct.; Bedford, County Record Office, Lucas papers 30/9/102/12, Yorke to Grey, 27 Oct. 1747; Sheffield City Libraries, Wentworth Woodhouse Muniments, M3 73, Lady Finch to Earl of Malton, 19 Aug. 1740.

21. BL.Add. MS 15,957 f.29, Sandwich to Anson, 14 Nov. 1747.

22. RA.CP. 32/245, Newcastle to Cumberland, 11 March 1748.

23. Black, 'Anglo-Spanish Naval Relations in the Eighteenth Century', *The Mariner's Mirror*, 77 (1991), 235–58; PRO, SP 92/59 f.170, Holdernesse to Rochford, 4 Oct. 1751.

24. PRO, SP 80/192, Newcastle to Keith, 22 Oct., Keith to Newcastle, 3 Nov. 1753.

25. N. Tracy, *Navies, Deterrence, and American Independence. Britain and Seapower in the 1760s and 1770s* (Vancouver, 1988).

26. Paris, Archives Nationales, KK 1372, Puysieulx to Richelieu, 22 July 1748; J.G. Droysen *et al.*, eds, *Politische Correspondenz Friedrichs des Grossen* (46 vols., Berlin, 1879–1939) VI, 218; PRO, SP 88/70, Hanbury-Williams to Newcastle, 30 July 1749.

27. *Sbornik Imperatorskogo Russkogo Istoricheskogo Obshchestva* (148 vols., St Petersburg, 1867–1916), vol. 103 (1897), 259–60, 275; D. Aldridge, 'Admiral Sir John Norris and the British Naval Expeditions to the Baltic Sea 1715–1727' (unpublished Ph.D. thesis, London, 1971); Aldridge, 'The Royal Navy in the Baltic 1715–1727', in W. Minchinton, ed., *Britain and the Northern Seas* (Pontefract, 1988), 75–9.

28. *Politische Correspondenz*, IX, 345.

29. C. Baudi di Vesme, *La politica Mediterranea inglese nelle relazioni degli inviati italiani a Londra durante la cosidetta Guerra di successione d'Aus-*

tria (Turin, 1952); Black, 'The Development of Anglo-Sardinian Relations in the First Half of the Eighteenth Century', *Studi Piemontesi*, 12(1983), 48–60.

30. *Craftsman*, 19 Nov. 1742; *Westminster Journal*, 18 March 1749; *Remembrancer*, 9 Sept. 1749; *Old England*, 9, 16 June, 6 Oct. (extract quoted) 1750.

31. Oxford, Bodleian Library, MS.D.D. Dashwood B11/12/6, Vernon to Dashwood, 29 July 1749, AE.CP. 426 f.299, Puysieulx to Durand, 7 July 1749. Mémoires et Documents Angleterre 51, ff. 144–5, 166, Réflexions de M. de Bussy, 19 March 1751, Mirepoix, Portrait de la Cour d'Angleterre, Nov, 1751.

32. For examples of British activity, PRO, SP 84/448, f.239, intelligence from Paris, 9 June 1748, forwarded from Liège to Duke of Newcastle, 98/54, f.65, Consul Birtles at Leghorn to Duke of Bedford, Secretary of State for the Southern Department, 12 August 1748; London, Bedford Estate Office, vol. 23, Bedford to Earl of Albermarle, envoy in Paris, 5 April 1750; BL, Add. MS 57,927, f.133, Earl of Halifax, Secretary of State for the Southern Department, to Under Secretary Weston, 2 Jan. 1764; Black, 'British Intelligence and the Mid-Eighteenth Century Crisis', *Intelligence and National Security*, 2 (1987), 209–29.

33. BL, Add. MS 35,363, f.324, Joseph to brother Philip Yorke, 13 March 1753; PRO, SP 84/463, Newcastle to Yorke, 26 June 1753.

34. PRO, SP 92/58, ff. 177–8, Rochford to Bedford, 1 Oct. 1749; BL, Add. MS 35, 410, ff. 153–4, Newcastle to Hardwicke, 10 Sept. 1749.

35. AE. Mémoires et Documents Angleterre 51, f. 141, Réflexions de M. de Bussy, 19 March 1751.

36. K.W. Schweizer, 'The Seven Years' War: A Systematic Perspective' in Black, ed., *The Origins of War in Early Modern Europe* (Edinburgh, 1987), 242–60.

37. BL, Egerton MS 3442, ff. 99–100, 122, 74–5, Cumberland to Holdernesse, 31 May, 18 June, Holdernesse to Cumberland, 13 May 1757.

38. W. Hackman, 'English military expeditions to the coast of France, 1757–1761', (unpublished Ph.D. thesis, University of Michigan, 1968); M. Peters, *Pitt and Popularity* (Oxford, 1980), 91–4; R. Middleton, *The Bells of Victory* (Cambridge, 1985), 26–30.

39. Mount Stuart, Bute, papers of the third Earl of Bute, 1761 correspondence Nos. 447, 478, Pitt to Bute, May, Bedford to Bute, 9 July 1761.

40. Black, 'The Crown, Hanover and the Shift in British Foreign Policy in the 1760s' in Black, ed., *Knights Errant and True Englishmen. British Foreign Policy 1660–1800* (Edinburgh, 1989), 113–34.

41. N.A.M. Rodger, 'The British View of the Functioning of the Anglo-Dutch Alliance, 1688–1795', in G.J.A. Raven and Rodger, eds, *Navies and Armies, The Anglo-Dutch Relationship in War and Peace 1688–1988* (Edinburgh, 1990), 12–32.

42. BL, Add. MS 57,927, ff. 298, 346, Edward Sedgwick, Under Secretary in the Southern Department, to Weston, 4 Aug., 6 Oct. 1764.

4

THE ESTABLISHMENT OF THE WESTERN SQUADRON AS THE LINCHPIN OF BRITISH NAVAL STRATEGY

Michael Duffy

In a previous chapter David Davies showed how concern had been expressed at French naval expansion ever since 1666, and three times, in 1666–7,1668 and 1678, English war planners had to face the actuality or threat of war with France. Yet while a strategy was devised for confronting the French danger, nothing was done to provide the essential infrastructure to support such a strategy. Charles II and James II spent their money on the tangible, instant power of a battlefleet rather than on the resources necessary to maintain it in areas where it had never operated for any length of time before. Although a citadel was built to strengthen the defences of Plymouth in the late 1660s, naval ships were only serviced there by a careening hulk, which remained thirty-seven years in the Cattewater until it was condemned in 1684, and by a Victualling Board agent operating out of rented accomodation at Lambhay. The only dry docking capacity and only dockyard in the Channel was at Portsmouth, where there were two dry docks formed as a double dock which could accommodate up to the smallest first rate ships of the line of battle. However virtually all the Navy's manufacturing capacity and the vast majority of its dry docking facilities (three double and five single) were concentrated in the great naval arsenals on the Thames and Medway, at Deptford, Woolwich and at Chatham with its dependency Sheerness.[1] This was the result of the needs of a series of Dutch Wars and also of the fact that London was the greatest manufacturing centre of the country (and indeed of Europe).

The consequences of this unbalanced naval infrastructure were rapidly seen when war broke out with France in 1689. The long feared French invasion of Ireland from their own great naval arsenal at Brest took place at once, and when the English squadron sent to contest it was so damaged in battle at Bantry Bay on 1 May as to be obliged to return to port, it had to put back as far as Portsmouth to make repairs. Because of the limited capacity of that yard it was nearly two months before the squadron could get back on station again.[2] In the meantime the French held the strategic initiative, operating from their naval bases at Brest and Rochefort to the westward and athwart the vital Anglo-Dutch shipping lanes to and from the rich trade of the Mediterranean, the East Indies and the Americas.

This time the response was rapid and decisive. The immediacy of the crisis which threatened the regime established by the Revolution of 1688 produced an identity of interests between the Parliament that supplied the money and the Monarchy that executed policy, so that a major and expensive restructuring of the essential dockyard support for naval operations was at last undertaken. A complete new dockyard, with a single dry dock and an enclosed wet dock, was established at Plymouth, and two new dry docks and two wet docks built at Portsmouth. The extent of the commitment was shown by the fact that the new dry docks were built to the most modern design in stone, which was considerably more expensive but far more durable and efficient than the wood used hitherto. Total costs were considerable—the work at Plymouth dockyard alone was valued at £67,095 6s 0d in 1698.[3]

Yet even at this stage there was still difficulty in formulating the right strategy to handle the French menace, and this was reflected in the new support structure provided. The expectation at the start of this prolonged period of warfare with France seems to have been that the main theatre of conflict would be in the English Channel, directly between the two warring countries, and this seemed confirmed by the first two major batttlefleet engagements, off Beachy Head in 1690 and Barfleur-La Hogue in 1692. In consequence the overall trend of naval expenditure in the 1690s-early 1700s was to create a main battlefleet base at Portsmouth rather than at Plymouth. The pattern became one whereby most of the battlefleet would be prepared at the start of the year in the Thames yards, and would then move out to pick up the Dutch contingent either at the Downs or at Portsmouth, which then acted as its operational supply and repair base for the campaigning season. There were indeed particular advantages for using Portsmouth rather than Plymouth. It was closer to London, which meant that orders and reports could be transmitted more expeditiously and that any deficiencies in victuals or naval stores or munitions could more easily be resupplied from the great manufactures on the Thames. Also at Spithead it had a sheltered anchorage in which a large battlefleet could be assembled, whereas

Plymouth lacked a secure fleet anchorage until the breakwater was built at the entrance to the Sound in the nineteenth century. By 1711 over half the entire dockyard labour force was still in the Thames yards, but Portsmouth dockyard had the single largest number of workers, a third larger than Chatham which was second, and nearly two thirds larger than at Plymouth which was fifth largest after Deptford and Woolwich.[4]

At this stage the role envisaged for Plymouth and the Western Squadron was still a subordinate one. The concept of a Western Squadron had existed at least as early as 1650 when Captain William Penn was appointed 'commander-in-chief in the western squadron' and charged with guarding the Channel from Beachy Head to Land's End with six ships.[5] The system was continued under the Restoration, with a Western Squadron of 6–8 warships, usually fourth, fifth and sixth rates, engaged in cruising and convoying, protecting British trade while also seeking to attack enemy commerce and commerce-raiders out as far westward as the Soundings. The squadron was based on Plymouth to which it had frequent recourse for careeening, since commerce raiding and commerce protection required fast ships, and clean hulls were worth an extra one and a half knots to a warship's speed.[6] The initial decision in 1689 to build a dry-dock at Plymouth capable of receiving up to third rate cruising ships was thus only a partial expansion of this role, and though in early 1691 the contract for the dock was upgraded to accomodate the first and second rate 'Great Ships' of the line,[7] the fact that only a single dry-dock was ordered still clearly implied that a yard capable of maintaining the main battlefleet for any length of time was not yet envisaged. A great many developments were needed—conceptual, institutional, logistical—before Plymouth dockyard reached the parity with Portsmouth that it achieved in the latter part of the French Wars and before the Western Squadron became effectively Britain's main battlefleet.

In the first place it took some time for the planners to grasp that the principal theatre of operations was not going to be in the Channel as they had envisaged. After (and perhaps because of) their defeat at Barfleur-La Hogue, the French did not send a fleet into the Channel again until 1744 and thereafter only did so twice more, in 1779 and 1781. This was because the prevailing south westerly winds made the Channel a cul de sac for them in which they had no naval bases capable of receiving first and second rate ships of the line. If these latter got into trouble either through damage from the elements or from battle then their chances of survival were low. After Barfleur these great ships had nowhere to hide and were destroyed in the open bays of Cherbourg and La Hogue. The French fleet was only likely to enter the Channel thereafter if it thought that it had a strong chance of surprise (as in 1744 and as planned in 1805) or if it was in overwhelming superiority (1779 and 1781 when it was joined by the Spanish). Otherwise if it operated as a fleet it soon manifested a preference for working to windward of its main Biscay-coast fleet bases, out in the western approaches, where it could both protect French overseas trade and intercept the British trade routes, and from which it had a sure path of retreat should it need to use it. For the most part they left the Channel uncontested. Over time it became apparant that, unlike Britain's former Dutch opponents, the French would not go out of their way to seek out and bring the British fleet to battle (unlike the Dutch they didn't necessarily need to), and that they often preferred to concentrate on commerce raiding or using squadrons strategically in support of their overseas empire.[8]

Consequently after 1692 the main theatre of naval activity moved westward, leaving the main British operational fleet base, Portsmouth, 210 miles north-eastward and leeward of the main French fleet base at Brest and further still from where the Brest fleet chose to operate. However it took time to appreciate this French switch and still longer to put the British fleet into a position to operate regularly there itself. That very much depended on the available support facilities.

The establishment of Plymouth dockyard, at which a second dry dock was added in 1719–22, made it easier to operate the traditional type of Western Squadron on a somewhat larger scale. Sir George Byng was allocated nine ships for the task in the winter of 1704–5, William Martin was given twelve in 1745. Martin's instructions would have been in no way unfamiliar to his predecessors. He was 'to command a squadron of His Majesty's ships to be employed in the Soundings and seas adjacent in order to protect the trade of His Majesty's subjects outward and homeward bound, to annoy the enemy's ships and commerce, and particularly to clear the sea of their cruisers and privateers... You are to proceed and cruise with the ships under your command thirty leagues South West from Ushant, with a liberty of stretching as far as sixty leagues, when you think it proper to do so, by reason of any advices you may get of the enemy, taking care not to be absent from your first station longer than ten days. ...we rely on your vigilance and care to keep at sea as long as possible, and to use your utmost endeavours to pursue the enemy, and to take, sink, burn or otherwise destroy them.' Martin's was still only a cruising squadron of third rates or less. It lacked the strength to take on the French fleet by itself and would need to be reinforced for this by first and second rates brought west from Portsmouth.[9]

To bring the main units of the battlefleet down-Channel, however, raised vast questions of maintenance and supply. Some of these emerged in 1705 when the very first prototype attempt to set up a Western Squadron on the later successful lines was undertaken. In that year the bulk of the Anglo-Dutch Grand Fleet was sent to the Mediterranean to help put the Archduke Charles on the Spanish throne, and there was much concern that this enterprise should not be disrupted by any sortie of the French fleet from Brest. Accordingly in May-June, Byng had added to his cruising squadron twelve larger units of the main battlefleet, subsequently reinforced by nine more. He was ordered to proceed off Brest, '..to use your best endeavours to inform yourself from time to time of the enemy's proceedings in that harbour and so to place yourself with the ships under your command, as upon consulting with the Flag Oficer and Captains with you, shall be judged the most proper for intercepting the enemy, should they attempt to come out and upon gaining sight of them, to do your utmost to come up with, take, sink, burn, or otherwise destroy them.' If the French got out and escaped him and there was dependable intelligence that they had gone to the Mediterranean, he was to send his second in command with fifteen of the line and two fireships after them.[10]

However, firstly, were the bigger ships of the line seaworthy enough for sustained operations in the Western Approaches and the Bay of Biscay? In the early French wars there was a strong feeling that the great first and second rates should not be out before May or beyond early September. Such feelings must have seemed confirmed in September 1691 when the 90-gun, second rate, *Coronation* was overturned by a storm off Rame Head when seeking refuge in Plymouth, and sank with the loss of all but 24 of her crew. When a savage storm devastated the shipping in Plymouth Sound in mid-August 1705, there were immediate fears for the safety of the first rate *Royal Anne* with Byng's fleet off Ushant. Byng in fact took his squadron back to Spithead, and successfully proposed that his one first and two second rate ships should not be sent westward again that year.[11]

In respect of seaworthiness, strategic possibilities were extended in the middle and late eighteenth century by improvements in ship design and an increase in size for vessels of comparable strength (see Table 1).

Table 1

INCREASE IN SHIP SIZES 1675–1803

	Year built	tons	name (guns)
First rates	1692(rebuilt)	1,568	*Royal William* (100)
	1737	1,921	*Victory* (100)
	1790	2,286	*Queen Charlotte* (100)
Third rates	1694	1,041	*Ipswich* (70)
	1759	1,574	*Hero* (74)
	1803	1,770	*Hero* (74)
Sixth rates	1695	256	*Biddeford* (24)
(frigates)	1740	448	*Rose* (24)
	1783	594	*Rose* (28)

Source: J.J. Colledge, *Ships of the Royal Navy*, (1987 ed.)

With first rates increasing by nearly a half, third rates by over three-quarters, and frigates more than doubling in size, they were all endowed with greater powers of endurance both in general seaworthiness and in their greater room for crews and stores. Also significant in expanding and prolonging seaworthiness was the sheathing of ships' bottoms with copper, initiated experimentally in the 1760s and applied to the fleet from 1779.[12] There is much still to be examined of the ways in which increased size and better design and construction of warships, as well as other technical improvements, expanded the parameters of naval strategy in the course of the eighteenth century, but one of the most significant was by enhancing considerably the capacity of warships to keep to the seas in most weathers and all seasons in the Western Approaches.

Secondly, even if the ships were seaworthy, could they be operated safely in the new western theatre? For a start, they were moving into unknown, uncharted and dangerous waters, particularly along the rock- and shoal-strewn western coast of France. The consequences of primitive and uncertain methods of navigation in western waters were highlighted by the wreck of Sir Cloudesley Shovell's squadron on the Scillies while returning from the Mediterranean in October 1707, and the Western Squadron was still losing ships on uncharted rocks off the French coast in 1804 when the 74-gun *Magnificent* and the 38-gun frigate *Hussar* were sunk. This was a difficulty ameliorated, but never totally solved, by experience and by charting while on station, getting more information as they went along.[13] But even the most seaworthy ship with the most reliable charts could not contend forever against storm conditions, and there was a need for a harbour of refuge, particularly against the prevailing westerlies, to stop a fleet from being blown too far off station. Plymouth was inadequate. The Sound was difficult of access in a storm and little shelter before the nineteenth-century breakwater was built, as was rapidly shown by the loss there of the *Henrietta* and *Centurian* on Christmas Day 1689. Byng's watch on Brest in 1705 was several times interrupted by the need to find shelter. Taking station in mid-May, a storm in early June led the Admiralty to expect that he had taken refuge in Torbay, though in fact he risked Plymouth. Returning again off Ushant, he was again driven back by contrary winds at the end of June, this time taking shelter at Dartmouth. Out again in July, he returned to Plymouth at the end of that month. Finally the great storm of mid-August drove him to take his squadron all the way back to Spithead for shelter and repair.[14]

Spithead was too far away to be a convenient resort and Hawke, watching against imminent invasion in 1759, was ordered to bring his ships no further eastward than Plymouth or Torbay.[15] However most other sheltered anchorages west of Spithead had limitations. Mevagissey Bay was thought too small and Falmouth 'clogged with many inconvenient shoales and suddain soundings'.[16] Cawsand Bay, at the entrance to Plymouth Sound was likewise too small. The narrow and rocky entrance to Dartmouth between high cliffs was too hazardous in bad weather. Only Torbay was wide, safe and commodious enough to accommodate a large battlefleet against westerlies, but even that was exposed to the risk of any sudden shift if the wind through south to east, embaying sailing ships and threatening to drive them on to a lee shore. Nevertheless Torbay, 135 miles from Ushant, was the closest and largest haven for a battlefleet, safer and easier to run back to in a violent westerly than any other closer English anchorage and better than any further east until Spithead. Because of the fortunate circumstance (for the British) that the exit from Brest faced due west, a westerly storm which drove a blockading fleet off station would also keep the French in port. The need was to avoid being driven too far off station so that, when the wind changed, the British fleet could get back in time to catch the French as they came out or to deter them from leaving.[17] Torbay for shelter thus became the essential complement to the facilities for supply and repair at Plymouth for extensive naval operations to westward.

Therefore increasingly in the course of the eighteenth century, larger warships could be put in the Western Approaches, with a better design capacity to stay there longer, with a growing cartographical knowledge of the area in which they were operating, and with what they hoped was a safe route out of trouble in bad weather by using Torbay as a bolt-hole. There were still, however, three further and major difficulties which also had to be resolved before a really powerful and strategically effective Western Squadron could be established. Could it be supplied with sufficient victuals (and appropriate victuals) to maintain the health of the crews so that it could remain operational? Could battle- or weather-damage be repaired close at hand quickly enough for a large Western Squadron to remain up to a sufficiently effective operational strength? And what was the appropriate strategy to make the most effective use of a powerful Western Squadron?

The problems of provisioning a major fleet are best expressed by comparison. When in June 1692 Admiral Russell brought 64 English ships of the line and 24 fireships into Torbay to reprovision on a cruise from Portsmouth to westward, his crews totalled over 24,000 men, making his fleet the biggest 'town' in Devon by far—the next largest was Exeter with about 14,000 population. There were indeed only three towns in the whole of England with over 20,000 population and still only sixteen a hundred years later.[18] There was only one place in all England capable of coping without too great difficulty if that size of population arrived on its doorstep unexpectedly—and that was London, the biggest city in Europe with about 600,000 inhabitants in 1700 and 900,000 in 1800. London had the supply network and food-processing capacity to absorb an extra 24,000 mouths, and it was where the Navy's main victualling factories were located and why they were there. However it then became harder to maintain that size of floating population the further it moved from the Thames.

Ships of course could ease their wants by taking on board as large as convenient a supply of preserved provisions at the outset of their service. On 15 June 1743, for example, Captain Edward Hawke was ordered to fit out the *Berwick* at Deptford for Channel Service, 'victualled with four months' provisions of all species except beer, and of that as much as she can conveniently stow, floored with water and stored accordingly.' Too many stores however impeded a warship's fighting and manoeuvring capacity and on these grounds Admiral Anson in 1758 urged that the Western Squadron in future should carry no more than three months' provisions. Equally there had to be a minimum reserve left at hand to enable a ship to stay out or pursue the enemy in an emergency, and Hawke was ordered in 1759 to ensure that his ships had never less than two months provisions on board. That however left a narrow margin of consumption before there was a need for resupply.[19]

To help meet this problem, sufficient barrelled stores had to be kept close at hand at Plymouth or Portsmouth to re-equip such ships as put back for refit, or to resupply the fleet whenever it put into Torbay (Russell in 1692 was revictualled with beer, beef, pork, biscuit, pease, oatmeal, salted hake, butter and cheese by vessels from Plymouth and Spithead[20]), or over the course of time to resupply the fleet at sea off the French coast, all of which required the establishment of a fairly sophisticated logistical organisation.

This, however, only dealt with part of the supply problem, for more crucial still was the need for fresh meat and vegetables to help avoid scurvy and keep crews healthy. This was a constraint which, during the first half of the French wars, effectively limited cruises to a maximum length of six weeks before commanders had to bring their ships back to restore their crews' health. Whereas the great London depots and Portsmouth could help supply the preserved provisions, if a fleet was to remain on station in the west for any time, the need for fresh meat and vegetables had to be supplied from South West England. For Admirals anxious to be back on station as quickly as possible, this meant supply in a hurry. Nicholas Rodger has pointed to the contract of the Exeter butcher, Richard Cross, in 1759, to supply 'good fat, well-fed ox beef' at forty-eight hours notice—and how on 6 June 1759 Hawke came into Torbay demanding 46,926 lbs of it![21] This put a great strain on contractors. Faced with the unexpected arrival of Keppel's fleet at Plymouth in July 1778, the fresh meat contractor at that port threw up his contract and paid the £500 penalty. However the Navy paid well and others were usually ready to come forward, so that within a fortnight Keppel reported that provisioning was very nearly completed except for beer.[22] Fresh meat at least took the form of large animals which if available might be moved fairly speedily under their own power to slaughter houses at the coast, but the demand for fresh vegetables was even more severe. In the Napoleonic Wars the contract with two men, usually described as 'gardeners' of Plymouth for the provision of such cabbage (stripped of roots and stalks), greens, onions (dry and green), leeks, turnips, potatoes and carrots 'as may be required for the use of His Majesty's ships in this port and the Channel Fleet at sea' required that these should be supplied in **twelve hours** after demand.[23]

The work of Marcus, Gradish, and Rodger has shown how this difficulty of supplying a large Western Squadron was faced up to and solved during the Seven Years War (1756–63),[24] but the solution was in fact initiated even earlier, during Byng's pioneering close watch on Brest in 1705. Byng had 10,065 men under his command—perhaps three times more than the traditional Western Squadron. On 2 July 1705 he was told that it was so important for him to stay off Ushant, to prevent the Brest fleet getting to the Mediterranean, that 'beer, water and refreshments' would be sent out to him to enable him to keep on station. Victualling ships were assembled with beer at Plymouth, Portsmouth and in the Thames to go out to Byng, and on 11 July two members of the Victualling Board were sent to Plymouth to hire ships and organise fortnightly supplies of beer and water, sheep and greens to be sent to his squadron. In consequence it was bad weather rather than the collapse of his crews' health which intermittently drove Byng from his station, and the Brest fleet did not escape.[25]

This was the same basis as the methods evolved in 1759 to enable Hawke to keep on station and which resulted, after over six months' close blockade, in his having less than twenty sick out of 14,000 men in his Western Squadron when he won his great victory at Quiberon Bay.[26] The solution was laborious and expensive: thorough organisation of depots, the ensuring of the supply of fresh meat and vegetables, and the provision of regular convoys out to the fleet off Ushant, as well as the efficient arrangement of rapid resupply whenever it came to Plymouth or Torbay, were the keys to this success. Yet it should not be taken for granted. To take small and heavily laden victualling hoys and brigs out to Ushant was a hazardous operation at the mercy of the elements,[27] only to be undertaken if there was some certainty of finding the Western Squadron on station, and without such a shuttle service much of the effectiveness of the system was lost. Repeatedly between 1755 and 1759, sickness had compelled squadrons cruising to westward to return to port, and the impetus of the methods employed between 1759 and 1763 was lost in the War of American Independence when yet again scurvy rates soared and fleets were forced to return to port incapacitated by disease. In a large part this was because the wider demands on the Navy overseas, as well as the presence of a combined Franco-Spanish fleet in home waters, meant that the Channel fleet was not able to establish the supremacy which would have installed a Western Squadron regularly off Ushant so that a steady supply routine could be created. That favourable situation was finally reestablished in the ensuing Revolutionary and Napoleonic Wars, particularly during the period of close blockade between 1800 and 1805, and in addition the Admiralty began to authorise the supply of lemons, which were discovered by experience to be the most efficient medical remedy for scurvy. In his *Medicina Nautica*, published in 1803, The Physician of the Channel Fleet, Dr Thomas Trotter, was able to state that '... the late occurances of the Channel Fleet have sufficiently established the fact that scurvy can always be prevented by fresh vegetables, and cured effectively by the lemon, or the preserved friut of that juice.'[28]

Until then every force sent to the west ran the risk of succumbing to disease. After experiencing three such cruises, the surgeon of the 90-gun *St George* described the losses in the Western Squadron as 'perhaps greater than what we suffer in any other part of the world, even in the West Indies, at the worst of times, not excepted.' At that point, in 1747, up-gunning and up-masting of ships, with attendant necessary increases in manpower beyond former complements, were proceeding at a faster pace than the increase in ship size, so that chronically overcrowded ships, unable to store proportionately more water or fresh provisions, and sailing on extended cruises in one of the dampest and wildest theatres in which the Navy operated, were particularly vulnerable to disease. Eventually larger, less over-crowded ships, with more space for more nutritious provisions, afforded better protections to crews against the most deadly ship fever such as typhus, which proved particularly devastating in 1740 and again in 1755–6, but as late as August 1780, when Admiral Geary returned to Portsmouth with 2,400 sick of scurvy from a ten week cruise in the Bay of Biscay, disease could have a fearsome impact in interrupting operations and placing immense demands on the hospital resources adjacent to the theatre of operations to restore the health of precious naval manpower without which the fleet could not operate at all. This vital support facility had also to be built up. When Lord Torrington brought the Anglo-Dutch Grand Fleet into Torbay in September 1689, his ships had just buried 500 men at sea and had 2,000 sick on board, whereas neither Plymouth nor Dartmouth could or would receive more than 300 sick each. At the start of his watch on Brest in 1705, Byng was warned by one of his captains of the totally inadequate hospital facilities at Plymouth. It took until 1740 for the Navy Board to start looking for land on which to establish a purpose-built naval hospital, and not until 1762 was a 1,200-berth hospital finally completed at Stonehouse. Sick landed at Torbay were still being quartered in appalling conditions with civilians at Dartmouth until 1800 when St Vincent had a 300-berth naval hospital built at Paignton.[29]

What of the next major difficulty—the ability of Plymouth dockyard to cope with the standard maintenance and emergency repair of an enlarged Western Squadron in order to enable it to keep up its strength and so remain on station. Did it have sufficient dry docks? Did it have sufficient reserves of naval stores? Did it have a large enough skilled labour force? Did it have sufficiently speedy communications with London to get decisions taken or deficiencies supplied in a hurry?

Even the last of these was an important and now often unappreciated problem. The Navy was a highly centralised organisation, and dockyard officers were allowed little discretion for independent decision but had to refer to the Navy Board. Proximity to London was thus an important advantage and a reason why Portsmouth rather than Plymouth was for so long the premier naval base in the French wars. In the 1690s it took at best six days for a letter to be sent between London and Plymouth and a reply to come back. To wait so long could significantly impede operations and some latitude to the men on the spot had to be coaxed from London. After some experience with the Western Squadron, Anson requested in 1747 that:

...to remedy the inconvenience of its being so great a distance from London, I wish their Lordships would please give me a Standing Order for all the ships of my Squadron to be cleaned and refitted as often as I shall send them thither for that purpose.[30]

In the crisis of 1759 another type of expedient was tried to solve the problem of decision-making at a distance, in that the three main boards which administered the Navy each established their own direct representative at Plymouth capable of taking independent executive decisions without reference back to London: for the Admiralty a base commander-in-chief, Commodore Hanway; for the Victualling Board one of its Commissioners, Robert Pett, and, intermittently for the Navy Board, one of its Commissioners, Digby Dent, to back up the Resident Yard Commissioner, Rodgers.[31] This was an expedient which seems to have worked, but the problem was eventually more effectually solved to the satisfaction of the London authorities by the speeding up of communications by improvements in road-building, mail coaches, and eventually the telegraph in the latter part of the eighteenth century.

It was as well that the communications problem in the way of permission to clean, refit or repair was overcome, for there was immense pressure for such services from ships operating in the Western Approaches. Both the tasks of commerce protection and pursuit of the enemy, as well as the hazards of sailing in the dangerous coastal waters of western France, put a premium on speed and manoeuvrability which necessitated ships in good repair and with clean hulls. Operating in the wild and open Bay of Biscay moreover exposed warships to suffering considerable damage from the elements, and the risk of such damage was further increased firstly as crews became debilitated by scurvy or typhus and unable to handle their ships efficiently, and secondly as the Admiralty increasingly sought to maintain larger warships in the theatre in the savage winter as well as the calmer summer months. Anson described in 1756 how 'Cruising in all weathers and often with tempestuous and contrary winds wears out the ships, the masts and rigging, and ruins the health and costs the lives of the seamen; it often disables a ship in a week which has been three months in preparing'.[32] In order to attempt such operations with any hope of success, an efficient dockyard close at hand was indispensable.

As regards the availablity of adequate dry-docking facilities, the problem got worse before it got better, as the original two dry docks at Plymouth found difficulty in coping with the expansion of warship size in the mid-eighteenth century. They were then however rebuilt and between 1749 and 1763 one was extended into a double-dock and a new first rate dock was built, followed in the 1780s by the 'Great Parlby Dock', the biggest anywhere yet constructed, capable of accomodating the largest first rate of any navy.

In naval stores, too, Plymouth found difficulty coping with the early stages of the dramatic expansion of the Western Squadron towards the close of the War of the Austrian Succession. In 1746 it ran out first of cables then of masts. In the following year, Anson was urging the need to 'keep an extraordinary magazine of all kinds of stores at that post during the war, and principally cordage, masts and sails', but by the end of 1747 the yard was short of canvas.[33] Thereafter however things improved. Four more forges were added to the smith's shop in 1748 to cope with the extra iron-work now being demanded.[34] Better management and better organised stock-replenishment got it through the Seven Years' War, and the big rebuilding of the yard from the 1760s onwards then increased its storage and fabrication facilities considerably. The vast programme of expansion and reconstruction drawn up in 1764, at an estimated cost of £379,170 1s. 2d. for Plymouth and £352,240 4s. 3d. for Portsmouth, took over thirty years to complete, and it shows the extent to which Britain's rulers had at last grasped the crucial import-ance of having a sound infrastructure of support facilities as the solid foundation to the power of its fleet. It may be significant of the demands expected on Plymouth that the expansion programme gave it the biggest ropery of all the Royal Dockyards.[35]

Manpower at Plymouth was also initially caught out in the first expansion of the Western Squadron, as the yard frantically saught shipwrights and caulkers from as far afield as merchant yards in Liverpool and Hull in 1747/8. Nevertheless the mid-eighteenth century increase in the yard's workforce was dramatic: between 1739 and 1748 it doubled, overtaking that at Woolwich; between 1756 and 1763 it overtook Deptford and Chatham to become the second biggest of the naval dockyards; and between 1778 and 1783 it reached parity with Portsmouth.[36]

The real test of these developments was whether Plymouth could handle a crisis. Usually the events of 1759 are used to show that it could (apart from its inability to supply Hawke's fleet with beer that would keep, of which the admiral ceaselessly complained). Yet crisis was really avoided at Plymouth in 1759 by good management. Hawke was given sufficient ships to operate a planned system of rotation, with small numbers returning from Ushant at a time for repair and refit, being replaced by others going back once completed. Good fortune and good seamanship moreover avoided excessive damage that would have re-quired mass emergency repair, and Hawke still felt that 'that place is certainly improper for three deck ships either to lie or to fit at' (the new first rate Union dock did not open till 1763).[37] Plymouth's only substan-tial emergency in 1759 was when Hawke risked bringing the whole Western Squadron into the Sound in mid- October to complete with water and provisions for three months. By using the crews of two ships in dock to load all the yard's vessels with stores, by mobilising ballast barges to carry out beer and water, and by using two launches and the Squadron's longboats with anchors and hawsers to warp the Victualling Board's storeships out of the Cattewater where they were weather-bound, the port commander, Hanway, was able to achieve the revictuall-ing in six days, despite continuing bad weather.[38]

The acid test however was not in 1759 but in 1778, when Keppel brought back his shattered fleet from the battle of Ushant, because that showed Plymouth's ability to cope with an emergency. When the incom-ing fleet was sighted at 7 a.m. on 31 July, the Yard Commissioner went out in his yacht to arrange with Keppel at sea what had to be done. All the yard launches came out to take the wounded to Stonehouse Hospital, since the fleet's longboats had been disabled in the action. The yard officers then had to draw up a rapid repair programme for twenty-three battleships. The most extensive damage was to masts and rigging, and the Master Shipwright with his mastmakers went round the fleet deciding what needed replacing and what could be fished and saved. Keppel added to their difficulties by refusing to bring his ships up the Hamoaze to the yard (since it was notoriously difficult to make the passsage out again quickly). Consequently the most lightly damaged vessels stayed outside the Sound in Cawsand Bay to knot rigging, patch sails and take in new yards and topmasts. Vessels requiring major mast replacement were brought into the Sound where the second rate *Blenheim*, which had been preparing for sea, was cannibalised of its gear to replace losses and turned into a sheer hulk to lift out and replace masts. Three vessels with shot holes below the waterline were brought further into sheltered water to be heeled over and repaired, and one leaking fireship and the most severely damaged battleship, the *Egmont*, taken into dry dock.

Just over two weeks later, on 15 August, fifteen ships were ready to sail, and Keppel finally got to sea again on the 23rd with all his fleet except the *Egmont*, which was expected to follow in two or three days. The whole repair operation took just over three weeks and it is interesting to compare it with that of the French at the same time. After the batle on 27 July, the French Admiral, d'Orvilliers, took his own, less damaged fleet back into France's main naval base at Brest, which he reached on the 29th (two days before Keppel reached Plymouth) and he did not get out again until 18th August (only five days before Keppel). Efficient repair at Plymouth thus largely nullified any advantage that the French may have gained in the battle.[39]

The crisis of 1778 therefore left little doubt that Plymouth could sustain a large and powerful Western Squadron which it had by then become. Some of the advantages of operating such a powerful force out to the westward were pointed out as early as 1693 when one of the Treasury Commissioners, Sydney Godolphin, urged William III that such a disposition would prevent the junction of the French Toulon and Brest squadrons, which was their main resource for establishing naval superiority, and that the Brest squadron would never venture into the Channel while it knew that there was a superior English fleet to westward (and windward) of it.[40] In 1702 Admiral Cloudesley Shovell echoed this last point in arguing the advantages of a strong Western Squadron 20–40 leagues south west to west south west of Ushant. There, further, it could intercept the Brest fleet if it tried to follow Sir George Rooke in his planned attack on Cadiz, and it might equally hope to pick up Chateau-Reynaud's incoming fleet from the West Indies.[41] However, besides the logistical difficulties of providing and ensuring the maintenance so far west of a force superior at all times to the French, it was still thought an unproven gamble to defend against threatened invasion across the Channel by means of a force stationed so far outside it to the westward, and neither the politicians, nor Shovell in 1702, nor Byng in 1708, were prepared to risk it. The successful 1705 undertaking was an exception, carried out in special circumstances to stop an enemy expected to venture out south-westward rather than into the Channel, but it did show again one advantage of a powerful Western Squadron: that operations as far afield as the Mediterranean could be defended by a force stationed off Ushant.

In the event, however, it was not until towards the end of the Austrian Succession War from 1746 and in the subsequent Seven Years War that the traditional small cruising Western Squadron began to expand. Why then?

In part, as has now been shown, it was because the means were developing to make it possible to do so, though indeed in many aspects the means improved to keep pace after the decision was made rather than vice versa. In part it was the inevitable eventual result of the general choice by the French of a western theatre for their operations that was mentioned at the beginning of this article, but two further factors had special play at this particular time.

The first was the very serious threat of a French and Jacobite invasion between 1744 and 1759—dangerous not just in the size of the potential invasion force but because no one knew how much internal Jacobite support the invaders might receive. This led to a reconsideration of the best way to contain the invasion menace. Admiral Vernon, who commanded the main force assembled in the eastern Channel to guard against the invasion force assembled at Dunkirk, was decidedly uneasy at having unwieldy first and second rates squeezed into such narrow seas where there was not room enough for them to drive in a storm nor harbour big enough for them to find shelter before the Firth of Forth. On purely practical grounds he thought them safer to the westward, where there was room enough to drive and harbours in Ireland, at Plymouth and at Portsmouth for them to run to. (It is interesting that presumably because of their greater size, the big three deckers were now thought safer out to the westward than in the Channel or North Sea!) But also on strategic grounds Vernon now argued that:

> ...a western squadron formed as strong as we can make it by the junction of these five great ships to those Admiral Martin has to the westward and what others can be spared and got speedily to the Soundings, might face their united force, cover both Great Britain and Ireland and be in a

74

condition to pursue them wherever they went, and be at hand to secure the safe return of our homeward bound trade from the East and West Indies...[42]

In this one crowded sentance are stated almost all the future functions of the Western Squadron.

The second important factor was the switch of the major thrust of the British war effort away from Europe, where it had been in the wars of William III and Marlborough, and into an overseas contest for imperial supremacy. In this new policy the Navy could play a major strategic role of more significant influence than it had exercised in the earlier French wars, by throttling France's ability to menace the British colonies or to protect its own. This role, Anson argued in a memorandum in 1756, could be most effectively performed in the Western Approaches:

> Our colonies are so numerous and so extensive that to keep a naval force at each equal to the united force of France would be impracticable with double our navy. The best defence therefore, for our colonies as well as our coasts, is to have such a squadron always to the westward as may in all probability either keep the French in port, or give them battle with advantage if they come out.[43]

In 1745–46 a number of damaging French expeditions got away which Martin's small Western Squadron was unable to prevent—especially d'Anville's squadron of nine of the line with 3,500 troops in June 1746 to Canada, which wrecked the planned British strategy for America in that year of an expedition to Quebec. The build up of the Western Squadron began when Anson took it over in July 1746 and in August he had 29 ships under his command including his 90-gun, second rate flagship, the *Prince George*, and sixteen other ships of the line. This enabled him to patrol aggressively against any opposition in the Bay of Biscay, and the results were seen in the naval victories of 1747. Hawke's Western Squadron in 1759 numbered 25 of the line including one first and two second rates. From being a subsidiary adjunct, based operationally on Plymouth, to the Channel Fleet operating out of Portsmouth, the Western Squadron now effectively absorbed the Channel Fleet. It was prepared each year at Portsmouth and then moved down to Plymouth as its operational base. By 1805 Admiral Cornwallis's squadron was being called the 'Atlantic Fleet', and stretched to 44 of the line, including thirteen first and second rates.[44]

1759 and 1805 loom large as years of threatened invasion when the utility of the Western Squadron was obvious for all to see, but this anti-invasion role after the mid-eighteenth century should not mask its many other functions that made it the linchpin of British naval strategy. Its part in commerce protection and commerce throttling was less glamorous but equally crucial to the success of the British war effort. But perhaps least obviously apparent to the public was its world-wide influence.

Such an influence can perhaps be most clearly appreciated from the major occasion when it was unable to fulfil that role—in the War of American Independence. As Tony Ryan has written: 'It was no accident that the great sea fights of the American War took place in non-European waters. It was the consequence of Britain's lack of control in European waters.'[45] Because the Royal Navy had to face the challenge of both the French and the Spanish navies (the latter perpetually underrated by modern historians), and because it was tied down to supporting the army's attempt to suppress rebellion in the American colonies, it was unable to set up a Western Squadron sufficiently powerful to dominate the Western Approaches. It was consequently unable to control the area which was the main transit route for coastal trade between Northern and Southern Europe, and the European hub of the great trans-Atlantic sailing routes.

This was corrected in the more favourable maritime circumstances of the wars betwen 1793 and 1815 when the Western Squadron again became the main guardian of empire and the central strategic reserve for the defence of British interests around the whole world. Its commander in 1799, Lord Bridport, was instructed that if the enemy detached part of their force from Brest then he was to follow suit and that 'Your Lordship will direct the officer commanding the squadron you detach to follow the enemy to any part of the world to which it may go as long as he is able to obtain information on which he may certainly depend of the route it has taken..'[46]

One of the advantages of the trend towards larger ships was that they could take on more stores. By 1800 the requirement for the ships of the Western Squadron was to take on five months stores so that if any French force escaped they would have the capacity to follow it wherever it went or wherever they thought it was going: given the large and exposed nature of the British empire, a quick reaction was all important even if it did on occasion lead to following up false trails. When Ganteaume got out of Brest for the Mediterranean in early 1801, Calder with six of the line was detached to the West Indies. When eight of the line escaped from Brest in February 1809, Sir John Duckworth was detached with eight of the Western Squadron for the commercially crucial Caribbean, to be called back at Madeira with the news that the French had only gone to the Aix Roads. Nevertheless even in these mistakes can be seen the function of the Western Squadron as the first and major line of defence for the empire.

Within this grand strategic role that evolved for the Western Squadron there remained to be determined the local strategy by which this powerful force should be deployed in order to gain and maintain control of the Western Approaches, and here debate revolved about the respective efficacies of close or loose blockade. This was strongly argued at the time and the contention has been carried on by historians ever since. For a long time historians tended to follow the teachings of Mahan that close blockade was the ultimate answer, but more recently Tony Ryan and others have redressed the balance by showing a greater awareness of the advantages of loose blockade and of the disadvantages of the close system.[47]

Over the years the claims made for close blockade have been exaggerated. It was not foolproof and it could leak badly, in particular in January 1801 when Ganteaume escaped, and in January and December 1805 when first Missiessy left Rochefort and then Leissègues and Willaumez got out from Brest. Indeed Admirals implementing a close blockade recognised that it might leak and that was why there were two essential components to the strategy. It was not just a matter of keeping station hard off Ushant so as to be certain of engaging the French if they tried to get out of Brest, because the Squadron might be temporarily driven off station. The other essential component was to try to deprive the French of the means to get out by exploiting Brest's weakness—its poor land communications, which made it dependent on supply by sea. Hence inshore squadrons sought to cut off all coastal traffic to the port. Close blockade was in fact designed less to defeat the French in battle (arguably Quiberon Bay was a triumph for loose blockade from Torbay from which Hawke sailed to victory) but rather to ensure that the French never put to sea at all. However the concentration of resources close up to the main enemy naval force limited the ability to exploit command of the sea against enemy commerce. The human and material price that had to be paid, moreover, was considerable. Having to stand so close inshore exposed ships to wreck, imposed an immense strain on the ships, their crews and commanders, and threatened in the long term to damage the Royal Navy more than its enemy.

Because it was so exhausting, close blockade in its full rigour was never sustained for more than two years at a time. Moreover when it was imposed this was for a specific purpose: either to prevent invasion as in 1759, 1801, 1803–5, or because in 1800 the combined Franco-Spanish fleet was bottled up in Brest so that, as St Vincent wrote, 'Upon the whole it seems to me the combined fleets are better in Brest than at sea with forty-eight hours' start of us.'[48] It was thus as much the circumstance as the admiral or any theory that determined the strategy. In the latter of the cases above even Lord Bridport, long thought a classic loose blockader, had tightened up his blockade from the time that the combined fleet reached Brest until he was relieved by St Vincent. St Vincent thereafter was off Ushant continuously from leaving Torbay on 27 May 1800 until he returned there briefly on 25 September, but other factors besides strategic considerations also led him into this policy. He was convinced that his crews would be healthier at sea than exposed to vice and drink in Plymouth or Torbay (and it says much for the improvements in revictualling that this should be so), and he believed that discipline, which he considered to have been lax in the Channel fleet, was best restored on active service at sea where, additionally, crews had less opportunity to contact each other and conspire as in the 1797 Spithead mutiny.[49] Close blockade was thus not seen as a general formula, to be applied in all situations, but rather as a particular response to certain ad hoc situations, not all of them strategic.

Loose blockade had the advantage of imposing less wear and tear on ships and crews. Both Keppel and Howe, who played distinguished parts in the 1759 close blockade, came to see the latter as only to be adopted in great emergencies and to prefer the loose system in its stead. Loose blockade took the Squadron out in a series of sweeps into the Bay of Biscay in the summer months, withdrawing periodically to rest and replenish in Torbay, while frigates off Brest watched the French movements and alerted the Squadron if they showed signs of sailing. In winter the Squadron stayed more in Torbay or Spithead leaving the frigates to continue their vigil. Cruising in this way gave more chance to exercise command of the sea against enemy commerce, while the greater opportunity provided to the enemy to put to sea gave greater chance of bringing him to a decisive battle. It also however risked their getting clean away, and Bruix's escape from Brest in 1799 was facilitated by Bridport's tendency to make long sweeps deep into the Bay of Biscay in search of prize money from commerce captures.

The system of close blockade was at its height in 1800–1 and 1803– early 1805, before starting to be relaxed again, with the Western Squadron sheltering more often thereafter in Torbay, Cawsand Bay or Falmouth, particularly in the winter months, and a sort of half-way system was achieved between the two methods. The Western Squadron was thus saved from disintegration under the strain of close blockade, but a more insidious threat then emerged as Napoleon began to devise counter-measures to nullify the effect of Britain's most powerful strategic naval weapon. A canal was built from the Loire to Brest to secure the supply of that base against the depredations of the inshore squadrons. The focus of western operations was moved further into the Bay of Biscay, to Lorient, Rochefort, and the northen Spanish ports, which were harder to watch, stretching the communications of the

Western Squadron to their limits and compounding its supply problems. What threatened most to undermine the British Western Squadron strategy, however, was that Napoleon pressed the building of first class fleet bases further eastward, up-Channel at Cherbourg and at Antwerp, where he built a new battlefleet which inevitably began to shift the focus of British naval activity eastward too. Fortunately Napoleon fell before a new strategy had to be devised. France lost the use of both the Spanish ports and Antwerp and its fleet, so that at what, though no one knew it, proved to be the end of the French wars (but not of many more war scares), Britain was still able to see the Western Squadron as its essential tool for naval supremacy. The last decades of the sailing era consequently saw its support infrastructure further strengthened at massive expense by the completion of the Plymouth breakwater at over £1,446,963 between 1811 and 1848, and the construction of the great new Royal William Victualling Yard at over £300,000 between 1825 and 1834.[50]

NOTES

1. J. Ehrman, *The Navy in the War of William III, 1689–1697* (Cambridge, 1953), 85–8.
2. E.B. Powley, *The Naval Side of King William's War* (1972), 134–43, 173–4.
3. J.G. Coad, *The Royal Dockyards 1690–1850* (Scolar Press 1989), 7–10, 92–7; B[ritish] L[ibrary], Kings MS 43, 'Harbours and Dockyards of England 1698' f.132ff.
4. R.D. Merriman, ed., *Queen Anne's Navy* (N[avy] R[ecords] S[ociety], vol. 103, 1961), 373.
5. H[istorical] M[anuscripts] C[ommission], *Portland MSS*, II, 68–9.
6. The Restoration Western Squadron is discussed by David Davies, 'Devon and the Navy in the Civil War and the Dutch Wars 1642–88' in Duffy *et.al.*, eds, *The New Maritime History of Devon*, I, (Conway Maritime Press) forthcoming. For warship speeds see D.K. Brown,'The speed of sailing warships 1793–1840', in E. Freeman, ed., *Les Empires en Guerre et Paix 1793–1860* (Vincennes 1990), 162.
7. BL, Lansdowne MS 847, f.5–v.
8. French dislike of operating in the Channel is discussed in M. Duffy, 'Devon and the Naval Strategy of the French Wars 1689–1815' in Duffy *et.al.,New Mar. Hist. Devon*, I, (forthcoming).
9. B. Tunstall, ed., *The Byng Papers* (NRS, vol. 67, 1930), I, 55–7; H. Richmond, *The Navy in the War of 1739–48* (Cambridge, 1920), II, 147–50; P[ublic] R[ecord] O[ffice], ADM[iralty Papers] 2/1331, Admiralty to Martin, 17 August 1745.
10. Tunstall, *Byng Papers*, I, 74–5.
11. Ibid., 90, 91, 93.

12. R.J.B. Knight, 'The introduction of copper sheathing into the Royal Navy, 1779–1786', *The Mariner's Mirror*, 59 (1973), 299–309. The 375 ships of the line built 1688–1755 averaged 1056 tons and the 261 of 1756–1815 averaged 1714 tons. R.J.B. Knight, 'The Building and Maintainance of the British fleet during the Anglo-French wars 1688–1815', in M. Acerra, J. Merino, J. Meyer, eds, *Les Marines de Guerre Européennes XVII– XVIIIe Siècles* (Paris, 1985), 43.

13. R. Middleton,'British Naval Strategy 1755–62: The Western Squadron', *Mariner's Mirror*, 75 (1989), 364. The loss of the *Magnificent* finally led the Admiralty to authorise an official survey of the approaches to Brest by Captain Thomas Hurd which he conducted in 1804 and 1806.

14. Tunstall, *Byng Papers*, I, 62–3, 78, 79, 83–4, 86, 91.

15. R.F. Mackay, ed., *The Hawke Papers* (NRS, vol. 129, 1990), 316.

16. BL, Sloane MSS 3233, 'A Survey of the Ports of the South West Coast of England'(by the Navy Board and Trinity House), f.37v. For further discussion of the search for sheltered anchorages see Duffy, 'Devon and the Naval Stategy of the French Wars', *New Mar. Hist. Devon*, forthcoming.

17. Mackay, *Hawke Papers*, 317, 337.

18. HMC, *House of Lords MSS, (1692–3)*, 14th Report, Appendix 6, 227–30, 232–3; P.J. Corfield, *The Impact of English Towns 1700–1800* (Oxford, 1982), 8, 111.

19. Mackay, *Hawke Papers*, 4, 212–3; Middleton, 'British Naval Strategy, 1755– 1762.', 357.

20. HMC, *House of Lords MSS (1692–3)*, 232–3.

21. N.A.M. Rodger,'The victualling of the British Navy during the Seven Years War', *Bulletin du Centre d'Histoire des Espaces Atlantiques*, II (Bordeaux,1985), 44.

22. PRO, ADM 1/94, Keppel's reports, 3,16 August 1778.

23. PRO, ADM 112/87, 15 November 1803.

24. G.J. Marcus,'Hawke's Blockade of Brest', *Jnl of the Royal United Services Institution* (1959), 475–88; S. Gradish, *The Manning of the British Navy during the Seven Years War* (1980), 140–71; Rodger,'The victualling of the British Navy', 37–53.

25. Tunstall, *Byng Papers*, I, 84–5; ADM 110/2, 11 July 1705.

26. C. Lloyd, ed., *The Health of Seamen* (NRS, vol. 107, 1965), 121.

27. PRO, ADM 1/802, Hanway 28 Dec.1759; ADM 1/92, Pt 2, Hawke 31 Oct.1760.

28. See BL, Add.MS 31,163, ff.16,93, St.Vincent 12 May, 11 August 1800, and its effect in C. Lloyd and J.L.S. Coulter, *Medicine and the Navy 1200– 1900* (Edinburgh 1957–63), III, 159; Lloyd, *The Health of Seamen*, 305, see also 249, 304, 307.

29. D. Baugh, ed, *Naval Administration 1715–1750* (NRS, vol. 120, 1977), 149 (see also Admiral Stewart's comments on the reasons for losses in the Western Squadron, ibid., 148, 152). HMC, *Finch MSS*, II, 240; Tunstall, *Byng Papers*, I, 79–80; PRO, ADM 174/288, Commissioner Vanburgh's Diary, 3 Sept. 1740; BL, Add.MS 13,173, St.Vincent to Spencer 19, 23 May 1800; Coad, *Royal Dockyards*, 297–301; Lloyd and Coulter, *Medicine and the Navy*, III, 159, 179.

30. PRO, ADM 1/87, Anson to Admiralty 2 May 1747.

31. See J. Marsh, 'The local community and the operation of Plymouth dockyard 1689–1763' in Duffy *et. al.*, *New Mar. Hist. Devon*, I, forthcoming.
32. H.W. Richmond, ed., *Papers relating to the Loss of Minorca in 1756* (NRS, XLII, 1913), 96.
33. PRO, ADM 1/88, Lestock to Admiralty 9 Sept. 1746; ADM 1/87, Anson to Admiralty 2 May 1749; ADM 174/14, 14 Nov. 1747; Baugh, ed., *Naval Administration 1715–1750* , 259; Marsh, 'Local community and the operation of Plymouth dockyard', *New Mar. Hist. Devon*, I, forthcoming.
34. PRO, ADM 174/14, 22 Jan. 1748.
35. Coad, *The Royal Dockyards*, 12, 199–201.
36. PRO, ADM 174/14, Admiralty orders 19 Dec. 1747, 23 Jan. 1748; D. Baugh, *British Naval Administration in the Age of Walpole* (Princeton, 1965), 264, 273–5.
37. Mackay, *The Hawke Papers*, 304.
38. Ibid., 317–23; PRO, ADM 1/802 Hanway 14 Oct. 1759.
39. PRO, ADM 174/116, Commissioner Ourry 31 July–23 August; ADM 1/94, Keppel 31 July–23 August 1778; G.R. Barnes and J.H. Owen, eds, *The Private Papers of John, Earl of Sandwich* (NRS, vol. 71, 1933), II, 128–9, 142, 148–52, 155–6; G. Lacour-Gayet, *La marine militaire de la France sous la règne de Louis XVI* (Paris, 1905), 132.
40. *Calender of State Papers Domestic, 1693*, 108; for discussion of early attempts to solve the problem of how to deal with the Brest fleet, see A.N. Ryan, 'William III and the Brest fleet in the Nine Years War' in R. Hatton and J.S. Bromley, eds, *William III and Louis XIV* (Liverpool, 1968), 24–48.
41. *Cal.S.P.Dom.,1702–3*, 193.
42. B.McL. Ranft, ed., *The Vernon Papers* (NRS, vol. 99, 1958), 459, also 445–6, 451–2, 532–3.
43. Richmond, *Papers relating to the Loss of Minorca*, 94–5.
44. Richmond, *Navy in the War of 1739–48*, III, 21, 38; R.F. Mackay, *Admiral Hawke* (Oxford, 1965), 200–3; P. Bloomfield, ed., *Kent and the Napoleonic Wars* (Gloucester, 1987), 100–13.
45. A.N. Ryan,'The Royal Navy and the Blockade of Brest, 1689–1805: theory and practise' in Acerra, Merino, and Meyer, eds, *Les Marines de Guerre Européennes*, 184.
46. H.W. Richmond, ed., *The Private Papers of George, Second Earl Spencer* (NRS, vol. 58, 1924), III, 296 n.1.
47. Ryan, 'The Royal Navy and the blockade of Brest', 175–193. See also R. Saxby, 'The blockade of Brest in the French Revolutionary Wars', *Mariner's Mirror*, 78 (1992), 25–35.
48. Richmond, ed., *Private Papers of... Earl Spencer*, III, 341.
49. BL, Add.MS 31,177, to Secretary of the Admiralty, 8 July; Add.MS 31,173, to Earl Spencer, letters of early June, *passim*, 5 July 1800.
50. J. Naish, 'Joseph Whidbey and the building of the Plymouth breakwater', *Mariner's Mirror*, 78 (1992), 37–56; Coad, *The Royal Dockyards*, 283–90.

5

'A LITTLE NAVY OF YOUR OWN MAKING' ADMIRAL BOSCAWEN AND THE CORNISH CONNECTION IN THE ROYAL NAVY

Nicholas Rodger

On 6th November 1756 Mrs Elizabeth Montagu wrote to her old friend Mrs Frances Boscawen with comments on the political situation, and on the possibility that her husband Vice-Admiral Edward Boscawen would again be included in the Admiralty Board, whoever formed the new administration:

> ...in these days of discontent, all are pleased with *him*, and I assure you it will discredit any new administration if he is excluded his share in it. No! that cannot, shall not be; it would put the very ocean in a storm, and the large continent of Cornwall into a rebellion.[1]

The object of this paper is to trace some of the connections between the ocean and the large continent of Cornwall in the eighteenth century. It is not yet possible to do this satisfactorily. We still know so little about the mechanisms by which the Royal Navy then recruited its men that it is difficult to study the subject in relation to any one county. No one would imagine that Cornwall was a typical English county, but in what it differed from the lands east of the Tamar we can hardly say in the present state of our knowledge, or rather, ignorance. What is clear is that many sea officers from Cornwall, and most notably Edward Boscawen, were very conscious of their identity, and very ready to identify and favour their fellow Cornishmen; moreover it appears that they used this connection to overcome some of the manning problems endemic to their service.

The Cornish Connection

Since these problems are still the subject of widespread confusion, it will be well to clarify, as far as we can in the present state of our knowledge, what they were. It is in the first place essential to understand that a ship's company was not like an infantry company; it was not a homogenous body of men with similar skills and responsibilities. It was a little society composed of men, women and children of different trades and professions, different ages and abilities, different social origins and expectations. The methods and circumstances of their recruitment into the Sea Service varied widely, and many diverse difficulties attended the process. For some, indeed many categories of a ship's company, there were no serious hindrances to obtaining the people required, and in time of peace it seems to have been unusual for ships to meet any difficulties at all, at least so long as they were not in a hurry. The manning problem was effectively confined to wartime, or, more exactly, to times of full mobilization, and it was virtually confined to a single component of the ship's company: topmen.[2] In peacetime when ships had little trouble recruiting their authorised establishment, the whole 'seaman' part of the ship's company (about sixty percent of the whole in a ship of the line) could be made up of able seamen, but strictly speaking this was a luxury when only a proportion of these men needed to work aloft. With enough men to fight their guns, men-of-war were lavishly manned by the standards of merchantmen. In such large crews the topmen formed an elite minority who could be supplemented, in wartime, by unskilled or semi-skilled men working on deck. Since virtually all the running rigging led on deck, all pulling and hauling was done below, and for this work many men, but few skills were needed. In the same way the majority of each gun's crew were needed, not to load or aim, but to haul on the tackles which ran the gun out ready to fire. Discipline, teamwork and time could make an efficient ship's company from men with little or no experience of the sea so long as the necessary minimum of smart young seamen was available to work aloft, and of experienced older seamen to serve as petty officers. It was usually reckoned that only one-third of the 'seamen' of a ship really had to be able seamen, with one-third ordinary seamen and one-third landmen; that is to say that only a fifth of the ship's company of a line-of-battleship, and an even smaller proportion of that of some frigates, needed to be real professional deep-sea sailors.[3]

The shortage arose from a fundamental fact, easily overlooked, which distinguishes the navies of the eighteenth century both from the armies of their day and from the navies of our own: they were demobilized in peacetime. This had many consequences, almost all destructive of fighting efficiency, but what concerns us here is the effect on manpower.[4] In an unregulated free market, seamen's wages settled at a level (or rather,

83

at levels varying between ports and trades) which ensured that roughly as many men worked at sea as there was demand for. Thus it has been calculated that before the Seven Years' War in the early 1750s, about 58,000 men were employed afloat, including the coasting trade and inland navigation. When that war broke out in 1755, the Navy increased steadily from a peacetime strength of 17,000 men to a wartime maximum of 85,000. At the same time the merchant fleet barely declined, and privateering generated additional demand.[5] With the wartime demand for seamen double the peacetime figure, it could only have been met if wages had risen to reflect scarcity, and if the supply had been extremely elastic. Neither of these was the case. Though wartime wages in merchantmen did rise steeply, there was no political constituency for an increase in the naval wage, which remained unchanged from 1653 to 1797. If it had been increased in wartime it would still not have overcome the inelasticity of supply caused by the long time required to train an able seaman. The true deep-sea sailor—which was what every naval captain was looking for—had invariably begun his career as a small boy and had reached the pitch of skill and agility needed to work aloft, when barely into the strength of young manhood. The process took years; at least two, it was generally reckoned, even for good recruits of the right age. In the best circumstances, the labour market for seamen could respond only very slowly to the changed situation of wartime; higher wages would certainly have alleviated the problem by drawing more men into the Navy, but how many of them would have been able seamen is more doubtful, and no amount of money could transform a ploughboy into a upper-yardman overnight.

The function of impressment was to provide the Navy with the necessary minimum of able seamen, especially topmen. From an economic point of view, it has been persuasively argued, the press attacked the inefficiencies of the peacetime labour market, squeezing unemployment and underemployment to exploit the existing supply to the utmost.[6] This paper, however, considers the recruitment of volunteers, and specifically recruitment in captains' and admirals' home districts. In an age when captains were largely responsible for filling their own ship's companies, they had everything to gain by exploiting whatever contacts they possessed to recruit the most, and the best, men they could find. It looks as though these personal contacts worked in several distinct ways. Firstly in the recruitment of seamen, captains seem to have drawn on contacts made at sea; essentially they were looking out for their old shipmates, and their shipmates' friends and relations, trading on their reputations as decent officers who would treat their men well, as skilled seamen who would bring them safe home through the perils of the seas, and as successful commanders likely to be able to offer prize money and the chance of promotion. These contacts with men who were already professional seamen, made at sea or by reputation, were only weakly affected by consideration of where the officers and seamen happened to have been born. It is usual to find that a captain's lower-deck followers are drawn from all over the country, if not the world.[7]

The recruitment of young gentlemen—meaning boys whose fathers' social rank or naval contacts entitled them to look forward to a career as officers—was certainly affected by geographical considerations among others. It is common to find captains taking the sons of their neighbours and countrymen into their ships. Equally often, however, the contacts were professional, political or even commercial. A captain might have several young gentlemen from his own country, but others might be the sons of friends, relatives and brother officers from far away.

Geographical connections were strongest, not surprisingly, when men were to be recruited from the land. Though the Navy was unable to keep up with seamen's wages in wartime, it offered wages, and even more conditions, which remained attractive to unskilled labour ashore. When able seamen were scarce and officers had to make up their numbers, they turned to their connections at home. Many of them were drawn from the landed classes and looked first to their own families' estates; those in particular who came from the poorer and remoter parts of the three kingdoms seem to have found there the most recruits. In this respect Cornwall can be compared with the inland parts of the North Country, with much of Scotland, Ireland, Wales, the Channel Islands, Orkney and Shetland.[8]

All these aspects of recruitment can be illustrated from the career of Admiral Boscawen. There is no doubt of his strong sense of Cornish identity, and of his continuing interest in his fellow-Cornishmen in the Navy. We should know more of exactly how many served with him, and how they had been recruited, if the muster-books of H.M. ships in his lifetime had entered the age and place of birth of recruits, as they did from 1765, but even so his Cornish naval connection is large and prominent. But among officers and seamen the Cornish were accompanied, and probably outnumbered, by men from many other parts. Boscawen was a popular officer whom men were anxious to serve with; they volunteered to transfer to his ship,[9] and his former shipmates were prepared to desert to get back to him.[10] It would be interesting to know what proportion of them were Cornishmen, but there is no reason to believe it to have been high.[11]

Among the large number of officers who followed the admiral, the 'little Navy of your own making' to which his wife referred,[12] there were certainly a number of Cornishmen. In 1756, for example, he had an unsatisfactory officer of his flagship replaced by Lieutenant Jacob Lobb 'who comes from the neighbourhood of Penzance. You approve, I believe', the admiral wrote to his wife, 'of my taking and encouraging good men of that part of the world'.[13] But at the same time he was taking and encouraging good men from many other parts. His flag captain, John Campbell (who in peacetime 'was with me in the yacht at Tregothnan') and one of 'my own lieutenants' George Balfour were both Scots —indeed the admiral was notably willing to patronise Scotsmen at a time when they encountered virulent prejudice from most English officers.[14] Other young officers followed him from as far afield as Minorca.[15] At the same time Boscawen took a interest in the careers of Cornish officers who were not really his followers. Richard Spry from St. Just in Roseland served under the admiral at several stages in his career, they corresponded in friendly terms and his success in 1756 gave Boscawen pleasure ('I hope they'll think the West Country good for something'), but the critical stage of Spry's career depended on the patronage of the Irish admiral Sir Peter Warren.[16]

Furthermore many of Boscawen's Cornish connections among the officers were political as well as territorial. Himself M.P. for Truro, and brother to Lord Falmouth whose political interests were so prominent in Cornwall, the admiral was closely involved in the electoral affairs of a county which in his day enjoyed the influence in national politics which flowed naturally from providing nearly eight per cent of the House of Commons.[17] An officer in his position found that his political and professional interests could support one another to mutual advantage. At Truro opposition was regarded as futile because, 'the majority of the electors here are so attached to the Tregothnan family by the behaviour of Captain Boscawen, and his taking some of their sons to sea with him';[18] and when the admiral 'wrote to Lord Anson to make the bearer of this a Lieutenant, he is very well recommended to me by Cornish friends',[19] the First Lord can have been in no doubt what sort of friendship was implied. But this same process operated also to connect the admiral and his brother with many men of influence in national politics who had no Cornish connections, and led him to favour their protégés as well. On a single day in May 1755 he promoted four young gentlemen to be lieutenants, all on political recommendations and only one from Cornwall.[20]

Where the admiral's Cornish connection was strongest and most useful was in recruiting unskilled men to make up for seamen. In 1755 and 1756 he had a large party sent from Penzance, 'stout fellows but all landmen'.[21] It is interesting to note, however, that these 55 men were mostly rated ordinary seaman rather than landman.[22] In principle an ordinary seaman was a man with about one year's experience at sea, but in practice the rating often covered men familiar with the sea but not with square rig, therefore useful in many capacities aboard a man-of-war, but unaccustomed to working aloft. In the Cornish context this suggests fishermen, or perhaps part-time fishermen. It may be relevant to note that the admiral had interests in tin mines in Penwith and Kerrier, the far western hundreds around Penzance, and he used his agent there to send the men's advance wages home to their wives, which may suggest that they already had some connection with him.[23] Perhaps they were fishermen and miners according to season, in the typical Cornish fashion.

What all this adds up to is that even Boscawen, with his strong sense of Cornish identity, recruited in Cornwall only as one aspect of recruitment which reached much more widely, and that it was chiefly with unskilled men that his local influence was most useful. As far as we know, this was typical of senior officers, though probably few were as popular among seamen, or as strongly rooted in their home counties, as he. His death in 1761, aged only 49, was described as 'an event that greatly affects this country, there being a vast number of Cornishmen whose bread, and hopes of preferment depended entirely on him'.[24]

He was not, however, the last Cornish officer in the Navy, and it is instructive to look at some his successors and their followers, both as a contrast with Boscawen's, and as an index of the Navy's changing methods of recruitment in the second half of the eighteenth century. As a first example we may take the almost forgotten figure of Captain John Stott. He is said to have formerly been Boscawen's boatswain.[25] He undoubtedly was a former warrant officer, but a master rather than a boatswain, and there is no confirmation that he had ever been a follower of the admiral. His crucial promotion to warrant rank came from Commodore Townshend in the West Indies, at a time when Boscawen was in India.[26] It is not clear that he had any real connection with the admiral, nor even that he was a Cornishman born, but he described himself in 1770 as having:

...resided for a long time past near Penzance and St.Ives in Cornwall, where by my acquaintance in the Fishery, I imagine I should gett a Number of Volunteers to enter with me for the *Juno*, who are good seamen.[27]

His new command the frigate *Juno* was commissioned as part of the 'armament' which marked the Falkland Islands crisis. Though on this occasion war was narrowly averted, the mobilization, and consequently the shortage of seamen, reached wartime heights, and in response to his proposal Stott was allowed ten days' leave to go to Penzance to find his volunteers.[28] He obtained sixty men, a quarter of those whose place of birth is given in the *Juno*'s musters, of whom 52 were rated ordinary seaman, and all but two came from places west of a line drawn from Helston to Camborne.[29] The first thirty he described as 'young fellows who were for the most part brought up in the Fisherys of this Country'[30]. He also reported that, 'by the great rains... most of the principal mines in the Western parts of that County were stopt, and many very usefull men might be had'[31]. The similarity with Boscawen's recruitment is very marked, and the possibility is certainly open that he had in some fashion inherited some of the admiral's interest in the far west of the county.

Stott's next command, however, the *Alarm* which commissioned in 1772, was manned under peacetime conditions, had no ordinary seamen or landmen on board at all, and only one man born in Cornwall.[32] Even his last command the *Minerva*, commissioned in September 1777 when seamen were already short, had only five Cornishmen aboard.[33] This suggests that even an officer with strong local connections, and the possibility of recruiting men with useful skills, had no need to exploit them in ordinary peacetime conditions.

Stott is nevertheless a link in a chain of Cornish officers, for one of the sixty men he recruited around Penzance in 1770 was the thirteen-year old Edward Pellew, rated Purser's Servant.[34] Pellew soon fell out with Stott and became a follower of Captain Philemon Pownoll, and we must turn next to this remarkable officer. In every generation of eighteenth-century British sea officers there were one or two who were distinguished as educators of young officers. Invariably they were frigate captains, for that was the only school of seamanship; eminent themselves for their mastery of their profession, painstaking in their care of the young gentlemen, they enjoyed a reputation within and without the Service which made berths with them highly desired. In the American War of Independence Pownoll was without dispute the first; Jervis called him 'the best officer, & most excellent, kind hearted man in the Profession', and when he was killed lamented that 'we have lost the best Partizan, if not the best officer under every line of description in the Service'.[35] Such an officer attracted young gentlemen from every quarter, but what concerns us is his recruitment for the lower deck. Pownoll was not a Cornishman;[36] his family was settled in Devon, where his father Israel was Master Shipwright of Plymouth Yard. With a fortune in prize money made during the Seven Years' War he bought the estate of Sharpham near Totnes.[37] When the American rebellion broke out he volunteered to serve (unlike most of his contemporaries with money), and was publically thanked in the House of Lords by Lord Sandwich, the First Lord of the Admiralty, not only for his public spirit in serving when there was no obligation on him to do so, but for manning his ship with volunteers raised locally.[38] The combination of popularity on the lower deck and local influence in the South Hams (Dartmouth was then among

Devon's largest ports) allowed him to man his ships even when other captains experienced severe difficulties. In April 1777 he wrote to Lord Sandwich describing himself as:

> ...happily situated in a fine ship & exceedingly well manned with all volunteers except fifteen landsmen I received from Admiral Amherst to complete my compliment not having time to do it myself.[39]

When he was killed in action in 1780 his First Lieutenant and favourite follower wrote to Sandwich that:

> The ship's company have lost a father. I have lost much more, a father and a friend united; and that friend my only one on earth. Never, my Lord, was grief more poignant than that we all feel for our adored commander. Mine is inexpressible. The friend who brought me up, and pushed me through the service, is now no more![40]

The grief-stricken young man was Edward Pellew, with whom we return firmly to Cornwall. Pellew was in fact born in Dover,[41] but he came of an impeccably Cornish family. In the early years of the war against Revolutionary France he was in the unusual, if not unique position of commanding a semi-independent frigate squadron in home waters, based not on one of the dockyard ports but on Falmouth, where his brother was Collector of Customs and the family had extensive interest.[42] Victor of the first action of the war, already famous as a daring and brilliant frigate commander, he was in high favour at the Admiralty and was allowed not only to raise large numbers of volunteers in Cornwall when he commissioned the *Nymphe* in 1793, but to turn them over as he moved successively to the *Arethusa* and the *Indefatigable*.[43] The *Nymphe* had 104 Cornishmen in her company, a third of the men whose places of birth are identified. They came from all over Cornwall, and were divided about equally between able seamen, ordinary seamen and landmen.[44] This shows a rather different pattern of recruitment from Boscawen's, resulting in a much more Cornish ship's company than he ever achieved. By the time the same ship's company, or large parts of it, had been turned over successively to the *Arethusa* and the *Indefatigable* the Cornish were reduced to 58, or one fifth, but with experience they had almost all become able seamen or petty officers.[45]

Pellew was almost certainly the last Cornishman, if not the last officer of any origin, to build up so formidable a following from his own county. 'The ship's company, who have been my faithful companions during the war', as he described them in 1796, were representatives of a method of recruitment which was rapidly dying.[46] It seems that during the American War about 230,000 men were raised for the Navy, of which the shore-based Impress Service raised 116,357, or about half. These in turn can be divided into 72,658 who were paid bounty as volunteers, leaving 43,699 pressed men. Recruiting by men-of-war or their tenders stopping merchantmen at sea, and direct recruitment by ships of volunteers ashore, accounted for the other half. In all cases these figures refer to individual instances of recruitment; the Navy lost so many men by desertion and otherwise that it had to recruit two men for every one borne on a ship's books, and it must be that in many cases the same men were recruited more than once.[47] It is not possible to say exactly what proportion of these figures represent men volunteering to serve with particular officers, but it must certainly represent a considerable part of the volunteers both ashore and afloat. It is certain that captains were individually responsible for raising half the men in the Navy, and consequently that their influence was bound to be felt in every aspect of recruiting. As Commodore Rowley wrote to Lord Sandwich in November 1778:

> Most of the *Monarch*'s men have been of my own getting and have been tried, and many of the men would not have come into the Navy if it had not been to sail with me.[48]

In such cases, the captain was not only supplying the Navy's need of manpower, but acquiring a great deal of independent authority in the process. He and his men were personally linked, while the Admiralty was beholden to him for his efforts.

As far as we can at present tell, this independence declined rapidly in the 1790s. The construction and maintenance of large private followings was coming to be seen less as a contribution to the Navy's manpower, more as a threat to the Admiralty's control of the Service, and Pellew's treatment was a personal privilege denied to less fortunate officers.[49] An analysis of a number of ships which commissioned at Plymouth in 1805 suggests that by then the ship's companies of big ships were virtually all supplied by the Impress Service.[50] Small vessels built locally still found a proportion of their own men, but the great majority of recruits, whether volunteers or pressed men, were gathered by a national organization under the direct control of the Admiralty. In such a system there was little scope for officers to recruit amongst their own connections. Not until the introduction of Continuous Service in 1853 allowed ratings to join the Navy as a career, and the modern system of manning ports tended to draw them from a particular region, were there ships in the Navy so strongly identified as Cornish, and never again was it the personal influence of a senior officer which made them what they were.

NOTES

1. Cecil Aspinall-Oglander, *Admiral's Wife: Being the life and letters of the Hon. Mrs Edward Boscawen from 1719 to 1761* (London, 1940), 224.
2. An excellent summary of the manning problem at the time of the American War is Roland G. Usher, 'Royal Navy Impressment during the American Revolution', *Mississippi Valley Historical Review*, XXXVII (1950), 673–88; see here particularly 680–1.
3. N.A.M. Rodger, *The Wooden World, An Anatomy of the Georgian Navy* (London, 1986) deals with these subjects in greater detail.
4. Other aspects are explored in N.A.M. Rodger, 'Mobilizing Seapower in the Eighteenth Century', to be published in a festschrift for Professor Jean Meyer.
5. David J. Starkey, 'War and the Market for Seafarers in Britain, 1736–1792', in Lewis R.Fischer & Helge W.Nordvik, eds., *Shipping and Trade, 1750–1950: Essays in International Maritime Economic History* (Pontefract, 1990), 25–42, at p.29.
6. Starkey, 'War and the Market for Seafarers', 37–38.
7. Rodger, *Wooden World*, 119–24.
8. Rodger, *Wooden World*, 153–8.
9. P[ublic] R[ecord] O[ffice], ADM 1/1478, E. Boscawen to Admiralty, 18 Aug. 1742; ADM 33/378, Pay Book of *Dreadnought*, 1742–44, SB 363–371; ADM 1/90, f.51, E. Boscawen to Admiralty, 28 July 1756.
10. PRO, ADM 3/49, f.214, Admiralty Board Minutes 30 Jan. 1744/5.
11. Traditional wisdom is unhelpful: on the basis of a sample of 276 men born in Cornwall taken from the ships' musters listed in nn.29, 44 & 45 below, I have to report that by Tre, Pol and Pen you may know only four percent of Cornishmen.
12. Aspinall–Oglander, *Admiral's Wife*, 218.
13. Peter Kemp, ed., 'Boscawen's Letters to his Wife, 1755–56', in *The Naval Miscellany* IV, ed. Christopher Lloyd (N[avy] R[ecords] S[ociety], vol.92, 1952), 163–256, at p.243. Kemp prints 'Penrose', but Lobb was born and lived all his life in Penzance: see J. Stott to the Admiralty 21 Dec. 1770, in PRO, ADM 1/2481; F. Holburne to the Admiralty, 12 June 1763, in ADM 1/939; and *London Gazette*, No.9544, 6 Jan. 1756.
14. Kemp, 'Boscawen's Letters', 243. Another example is Philip Patton, for whom see Sir J.K. Laughton, ed., *Letters and Papers of Charles, Lord Barham* (NRS, vols 32, 38 & 39, 1906–10), II, 369.
15. PRO, ADM 1/1478, E. Boscawen to Admiralty, 8 Mar. 1741/2.
16. Kemp, 'Boscawen Letters', 241; Laurence O'Toole, *The Cornish Captain's Tale* (Redruth, 1986), 82; Julian Gwyn, ed., *The Royal Navy and North America: The Warren Papers 1736–1752*, (NRS, vol.118, 1973), 172, 440.
17. Sir Lewis Namier, *The Structure of Politics at the Accession of George III* (London, 2nd ed. 1957), 62, 299.
18. Namier, *Structure of Politics*, 127.
19. PRO, ADM 1/90, f.55, E. Boscawen to Admiralty, 4 Aug. 1756.
20. Kemp, 'Boscawen Letters', 179–80.
21. Kemp, 'Boscawen Letters', 174.
22. PRO, ADM 36/6187, Muster of *Northumberland*, 1755, SLVO.

23. PRO, PROB 11/862, f.50, Will of Edward Boscawen; Kemp, 'Boscawen Letters', 177, 196–7.
24. Sir Lewis Namier & John Brooke, *The History of Parliament: The House of Commons 1754–90* (3 vols, London, 1964,), II, 103.
25. Edward Osler, *The Life of Edward Viscount Exmouth* (London, 1941 ed.), 8.
26. PRO, ADM 107/4, p.410, Lieutenant's Passing Ceritificate; ADM 106/2897, pp.200 & 426, Succession Book. His biography in John Charnock, *Biographia Navalis* (6 vols, London, 1794–8), VI, 343, is not very informative.
27. PRO, ADM 1/2481, J. Stott to Admiralty, 23 Oct. 1770.
28. Admiralty Board minute, quoted in Ruddock F. Mackay, ed., *The Hawke Papers, A Selection 1743–1771* (NRS, Vol.129, 1990), 466.
29. PRO, ADM 33/522, Pay Book of *Juno*, 1770–72.
30. PRO, ADM 1/2481, Stott to Admiralty, 17 Nov. 1770.
31. Ibid, Stott to Admiralty, 21 Dec. 1770.
32. PRO, ADM 33/479 & 486, Pay Books of *Alarm*, July 1772 – Oct. 1775.
33. PRO, ADM 34/486, Pay Book of *Minerva*, Sept. 1777 – Aug. 1778.
34. PRO, ADM 33/522, SB 178/286.
35. British Library, Add.MS 29,914, ff.140, 143, J. Jervis to Mrs M.Ricketts, 19, 26 June 1780.
36. John Bannister, *A Glossary of Cornish Names* (Truro, 1871), 117, 134, offers a precarious Cornish derivation of Pownall as a form of Parnall; Edward Locker (National Maritime Museum: CLU/8) describes him as 'a Gentleman of American extraction'; but the name is usually derived from the place in Cheshire.
37. D.& S. Lysons, *Magna Britannia* (6 vols, London, 1822), VI, 15.
38. William Cobbett, ed., *The Parliamentary History of England* (36 vols, London, 1806–20), XVIII, 1261.
39. N[ational] M[aritime] M[useum], Sandwich Papers, SAN/F/10/78.
40. Osler, *Exmouth*, 45.
41. In the *Juno's* pay book (PRO, ADM 33/522, SB 178/286) he is described as born in Penzance and aged 16 at entry; more accurately he was aged 13 and lived in Penzance.
42. C. Northcote Parkinson, *Edward Pellew, Viscount Exmouth, Admiral of the Red* (London, 1934), 104–5.
43. Parkinson, *Pellew*, 96, 115, 213.
44. PRO, ADM 35/1177, Pay Book of *Nymphe*, Jan.– Dec. 1793.
45. PRO, ADM 85/844, Pay Book of *Indefatigable*, Dec. 1794– Feb. 1796.
46. J.S. Corbett & H.W. Richmond, eds, *The Private Papers of George, Second Earl Spencer* (NRS, vols.46, 48, 58 & 59, 1913–24), I, 246–7. For changing methods of recruiting see Rodger, 'Devon Men and the Navy'.
47. Usher, 'Royal Navy Impressment', 677–82.
48. NMM, SAN/F/17/8.
49. N.A.M. Rodger, 'Shipboard Life in the Georgian Navy, 1750–1800: The Decline of the Old Order ?', to appear in the proceedings of a conference held at Stavanger, August 1989, ed. Lewis F. Fischer & Helge Nordvik.
50. Rodger, 'Devon men and the Navy', Tables 8–10.

6

NAVAL POWER, STRATEGY AND FOREIGN POLICY 1775-1791

Jeremy Black

Fleets employed to cover a coast, are not only precarious in their exertions, which depend much on winds, but are miserably confined as to all the effects of naval war. Those effects are only felt when our fleets can keep the sea, in order to protect our commerce, and annoy that of our enemies, as well as to defend our distant possessions, and to cover descents and continual incursions. Such objects, however, cannot be pursued, nor can we in wisdom hazard anything, whenever the state of our internal defence is such as to require the presence of our fleets for the protection of our dock-yards, of our ports, and even of our metropolis.
(William Eden MP., Under-Secretary of State 1772-8, Commissioner for conciliation with America, 1778-9, 1779)

Britain wishes to fight with all the world. She is a marine Hercules who seeks to surpass with her tasks all that legend ascribes to the Greek Hercules.
(Frederick the Great, 11 March 1782)[1]

The period 1775-91 witnessed the worse defeats for British naval power in the eighteenth century and some of its most impressive achievements. Britain was involved in one major war and a number of confrontations with powers that were 'Continental' and yet also, to various degrees, dependent on or exposed to naval power: France, Spain, Russia and the Thirteen Colonies. The efficacy of seapower against a major Continental adversary depended upon the situation of that power, its ambitions and its other adversaries, and the measure of that efficacy must almost always be modest or worse if the strategic expectations were excessive or impatient.

During the Anglo-French stage of the War of American Independence (1778-83), the British were unable to maintain continual control of Caribbean and American waters, while in 1779 control of the Channel was itself challenged by a Franco-Spanish fleet.[2] It was not of course the case that absolute control was gained or lost; rather there was a relative decline in British ability to use the sea in a situation of contested control. Loss of naval control exposed British garrisons to attack (Savannah in 1779), or the threat of attack (New York in 1778), and played a crucial role in Cornwallis's surrender at Yorktown in 1781. Conversely, the Navy's achievements during that war included outfighting its Bourbon rivals, so that both France and Spain were pleased to see an end to the conflict,[3] and specifically defeating the Bourbon naval threats to Gibraltar and Jamaica. After the conflict, a stronger British Navy[4] played a major role in intimidating rivals, France in the Dutch crisis of 1787 and, more obviously, Spain in the Nootka Sound crisis of 1790,[5] before failing to achieve the same result against Russia in the Ochakov crisis of 1791.[6]

These contrasting successes and failures can be approached from a number of angles. The 'naval' dimension which would stress naval strength and preparedness has to be supplemented by the 'political' perspective, the questions of what naval power was supposed to achieve, how feasible the objectives were and crucially the interrelationship between British power and the views and strength of other states, both allies and enemies.

In many respects, it was this last factor that was indeed crucial. Britain was outnumbered by between 20 and 50 ships of the line in 1779–82. Two developments had threatened the naval hegemony that Britain had enjoyed in European waters in the first three decades of the century. The first was the recovery of French and Spanish naval strength, the second the increasing degree of cooperation between the two powers. The Foxite MP, Charles Howard, Earl of Surrey, told the Commons in January 1786 that:

...by maintaining our naval strength, he hoped it was not meant, the confining our Navy to its present establishment, or governing it by what it was in 1748, or at the end of the war before the last; but that, keeping in view the number and strength of the Navy of the House of Bourbon, we should take care to make our marine prove at least equal to theirs; since upon that circumstance alone depended our security.

Neither development was continuous nor without serious setbacks[7], and this provided the British with crucial assistance during the mid-century conflicts with France and Spain between 1739 and 1763. Having crushed France and severely defeated Spain as trans-oceanic powers in the Seven Years' War, the British appeared by 1763 to have recovered the maritime hegemony they had wielded half a century earlier in the aftermath of the War of the Spanish Succession. The situation, however, was more serious. Between 1713 and the negotiation of the First Family Compact in 1733, relations between France and Spain had rarely been close. They had fought one war, that of the Quadruple Alliance, which entailed Franco-Spanish hostilities in 1719–20 and had also been divided by hostile diplomatic alignments, most obviously in 1716–18, 1725–9 and 1731–3. This owed much to the persistence of the Anglo-French alliance, which lasted from 1716 to 1731. This advantage for British diplomacy was matched by naval strength. After the neglect or destruction of much of their naval power during the War of the Spanish Succession, only Spain of the Bourbon powers made a major effort to rebuild her naval strength, but this process was wrecked by her defeat at British hands off Cape Passaro in 1718. 17 ships were captured, 8 burnt.[8] What has been called by George Modelski and William Thompson the British 'relative capability share' of naval power was not challenged seriously until the 1730s, when the rise in the number of French warships during the previous decade was matched by a fresh growth in Spanish strength.[9]

The situation after 1763 was less promising. The most recent survey of Bourbon naval reconstruction has discerned failure:

...this failure to attain the target of 80 ships of the line initially set in 1763 was inevitably reflected in the significant change in French strategy which becomes visible by the mid-1760s, when the parallel attempts of Spain to rebuild her shattered Navy were seen to have been even less successful... Choiseul was forced to concede by the mid-1760s that the slow pace of French naval reconstruction and the negligible success achieved by parallel Spanish efforts were undermining his plan for a war of revenge... the preoccupation with naval reconstruction did not continue after 1766.[10]

This failure can be related to Britain's success in her colonial confrontations with the Bourbons in 1764–5.[11] Nevertheless, even if Choiseul's ambitions were not realised, the increase in the number of Bourbon warships was of consequence. That of French ships of the line rose from under 50 in 1763 to 62 in 1766, a number which France could safely man, while for Spain the increase was from 37 to 51 by 1770. This laid the groundwork for French maritime strength in the War of American Independence, and was supplemented by administrative improvements, though the strength of French naval administration should not be exaggerated.[12] The contrast with the situation after 1713 was readily apparent and, from the British point of view, there were two additional problems. First, Franco-Spanish relations, although not without serious problems, were closer than they had been after 1713 or after the Treaty of Aix-la-Chapelle (1748) had brought to an end the previous bout of Anglo-Bourbon conflict. Secondly, the British were given no opportunity to defeat one of their potential opponent's navies. There was to be no repetition of Passaro. In this simple military context the fact that the British achieved their objectives in 1764–5 without fighting was disadvantageous in the long-term, as was the Spanish decision to back down in the Falkland Islands crisis of 1770. Indeed, had the latter crisis broadened into a full-scale Anglo-Bourbon conflict, with France coming to the aid of her Spanish ally, then Britain would have found herself in a better military position than she was to be in 1778–83. Far from having to devote major military resources to the war with the American colonists and the related need to defend nearby colonies, Canada, Nova Scotia and the Floridas, Britain could have sought to harness American energies and resources to a war of conquest against Spain's Caribbean and American possessions. The energies of Massachusetts could have been directed towards expeditions agianst Havana and New Orleans, though it would have entailed a redirection of the North government's American policy in order to obtain the colony's cooperation. The British naval mobilisation in 1770 was indeed impressive[13], and, given that war with the Bourbons was to break out in less than a decade, it is arguable that the British would have been fortunate to fight in 1770; just as an Anglo-French conflict arising from the Nootka Sound crisis of 1790 would probably have had very beneficial consequences for the British during the French Revolutionary War.

This argument cannot be pushed too far. The danger of assuming military inevitability is readily apparent. In 1755 hopes that Boscawen would be able to defeat the French fleet sailing to reinforce French Canada had been sadly disappointed. Although it is commonly assumed that Britain would have triumphed in any war restricted to naval and colonial operations, recent experience was ambigious, and the limited success of amphibious operations against Spain in the Caribbean during the War of Jenkins's Ear was especially notable.[14] The Anglo-French struggle during the Seven Years' War had not seen British troops committed to the continent until 1758, and Spain had not entered the war on the side of France until 1762. Nevertheless, 1756–7 were scarcely years of British maritime triumph. In 1756 Byng's attempt to relieve Minorca had failed; in 1757 the expedition designed to seize Louisbourg had been unsuccessful. Simply by keeping their fleet in being and threatening invasion, as in 1756, the French could largely determine British strategy, though the British were the superior power, and not without some freedom of movement. It was not an inability to take the initiative which caused the 1757 Louisburg project to fail.

Even had Britain been more fortunate in any war in 1770–1, it is dangerous to abstract military conjectures from their political context. Any conflict would have created serious financial strains, although

Britain succeeded in confronting the massive financial challenge of the War of American Independence, the French Revolutionary and the Napoleonic wars. Domestically, it would not have been difficult to obtain support for war with the Bourbons in 1770–1, although it is not clear how easy it would have been to sustain it had the conflict been less than successful. No general election was due until 1775. The international context was more problematic. A French military threat to Hanover, as in 1741 and 1757, could not have been parried militarily or politically.

Hypothetical arguments are dangerous, although of course contemporary commentators resorted to them constantly in defining the parameters of possible developments. The Falkland Islands crisis was important because it did not give the British an opportunity to crush their opponents' naval power. Indeed, it left them with an exaggerated sense of their naval potential, and thus prefigured the impact of the Nootka Sound crisis. Just as expectations engendered by the latter were to be proved misplaced during the Ochakov crisis, so the War of American Independence proved a salutary shock to those who had neglected the lessons of British naval limitations that the mid-century Anglo-Bourbon wars offered, and had instead propagated in the press a notion of maritime invincibility.

The limitations of naval power in the American crisis, given the then size of the British Navy, had been revealed prior to Bourbon entry. The concentration of naval vessels in Boston harbour and along the New England coast, as occurred in 1774–5, was only achieved by leaving the rest of the American coast largely unsupervised, and thus permitting trade to continue essentially without restrictions. Once war had broken out, the Navy proved unable to protect trade from American privateers, in American, Caribbean, Nova Scotian and European waters.[15] It also failed to block the crucial supply of French munitions to the American revolutionaries.[16]

Such tasks were arguably beyond the capability of any eighteenth-century Navy. The task of blockading fleets of ships of the line, which could only operate from a restricted number of ports, was difficult enough. Dealing with individual merchantmen and privateers was far more difficult. There is an interesting parallel with the problem that the British army encountered in protecting Loyalists from their Revolutionary opponents. In great part, the Loyalists had to be left to their own devices, while the army garrisoned major posts and prepared for field-engagements. The British Navy essentially did not have the comparable task prior to France's entry into the war, because the continental Navy of the Revolutionaries was not a formidable force. Not large enough for fleet actions, it made less of a contribution to the Revolutionary war-effort than the privateers.[17] On the other hand, naval options were limited dramatically by the need to support the operations of the army.

This was, of course, in keeping with the general pattern of amphibious operations at the expence of France and Spain earlier in the century. There were, however, important differences. During the Seven Years' War, the British were essentially obliged in their colonial warfare to defeat small armies composed of regular European units supported by native irregulars. Campaigns centred on the capture of major fortresses and centres of government, such as Louisbourg and Quebec, most of which could be reached by sea. Most of the British targets were island bases, such as Louisbourg, Guadeloupe and Martinique, or isolated coastal bases that had no real political links with their hinterlands, such as Goree and Pondicherry.[18] Faced by an attacking force enjoying command of the seas, these bases were vulnerable to any attacker able and willing to mount a conventional siege. Operations in the hinterlands of fortresses were limited. In 1762 the British captured Manila and Havana from the Spaniards, not the Philippines or Cuba, but these bases gave effective political and military control of what Britain sought, bargaining counters for the eventual peace treaty. The whole of French Canada fell into British hands with the surrender of Montreal in 1760. Had Britain, as planned, captured New Orleans, then Louisiana would have fallen.

Such a strategy clearly subordinated naval power to the exigencies of amphibious operations. Seeking to mount a permanent blockade of Bourbon ports in order to prevent privateering or other activities was an alternative use of naval strength, but it was not one that offered anything in terms of the economy of gains and losses that would determine the terms of the eventual peace, although in 1748 the impact of British maritime strength on French trade helped to encourage the French to offer moderate terms. In the pre-Bourbon stage of the American war the Navy readily fulfilled its task of supporting the army. Substantial reinforcements were moved to Boston in 1775, the army was evacuated to Halifax and then transported to New York in 1776 while Quebec was relieved the same year.[19] In 1777 Howe's force was transported to the Chesapeake.

Each of the tasks placed major burdens on British naval resources, and yet it can be argued that the British did not achieve enough. This argument seems plausible not so much in terms of the failure to prevent American privateering or to block their supplies from Europe, which, as already indicated, were very difficult tasks, but rather that British naval power was not used more extensively for offensive operations along the Atlantic seaboard.

Two counter-arguments can be advanced. First, one such expedition was attempted. It was planned that it should sail from Cork for Cape Fear in early December 1775, restore royal authority in North Carolina, where there were many Loyalists, and then join the major force under Howe as early in the spring as possible. The plan was not without value. Rather than pitting British troops against the hostile population of New England, it made sense to try to intervene in the more volatile and favourable situation in North Carolina. Had the arrival of the force been coordinated with the rising by the Loyalists there, it might have divided the south and crucially encouraged Loyalists in South Carolina and Georgia. The plan was unduly optimistic about timing, but the British enjoyed the naval superiority that enabled them to plan how best to employ the troops they were transporting to America, and the failure of Burgoyne and Howe to use the British army at Boston to effect suggested that bold measures elsewhere were required.

As it was, bad weather and administrative deficiencies fatally delayed the expedition, which arrived off Cape Fear in late April and early May 1776, too late to help the Loyalists, who had been defeated at Moore's Creek Bridge on 27 February. The British commander, Clinton, was then persuaded to attack Sullivan's Island, a sandspit which protected the harbour of Charleston, the most important port in the south. The attack, mounted on 28 June, was a failure. Clinton was unable to move his troops onto Sullivan's Island, because the water between it and Long Island was deeper than reported. Clinton noted that 'when many rivers fall into a sandy bay, new channels are formed every tide, and those which have 3 inches today may have thirteen feet tomorrow'.

The task was therefore left to the Navy under Sir Peter Parker. He determined to destroy the fort on the island by gunfire alone, but its 16 feet thick earth walls, faced by palmetto logs, were not badly damaged, and the well-aimed thirty heavy cannon in the fort inflicted heavy damage and 225 casualties. Clinton blamed the Navy for the failure:

The attack was advised on a supposition that there was water enough close to the ... Fort ... instead of going within 100 yards, as the pilot in my presence told them they might, they were by all accounts I have ever heard, not within 800 yards, no grape shot, no small arms, no fire from tops; in short they saw the scrape they were in, and would have drawn off, if the tide had permitted. The rebel fire was slackened a litte for want of ammunition, but it was renewed again, and so hot, that the ships were glad to cut their cables and steer away to their former stations.

Clinton's claim that had the frigates closed in and the army been able to attack, the British might have succeeded, can be qualified by pointing out that three ships ran aground, one, which could not be got off, having to be burnt.[20]

The second counter-argument is that attacking the American coastline would have had a detrimental effect on American opinion. On 18 October 1775 naval bombardment, supported by marines, destroyed most of Falmouth (now Portland, Maine). This inspired bitterness on the American part and contributed to their growing literature about British atrocities. Thus, the argument about how British troops should conduct themselves, in particular concerning how best to preserve and encourage Loyalist sentiment, can be seen to have had a naval echo. This was less serious an issue for naval commanders, as their usual operations did not bring them into contact with American civilians to the same extent as their army counterparts, and as they were not as dependent on local communities for their supplies. Nevertheless, local shortages of food were important to the Navy too, especially in 1775–6. The shortage of frigates for use in North America was a serious factor affecting British operations.

Despite these considerations, it can still be argued that naval power could have been used more effectively and in a more *politically* acute fashion prior to the entry of the French and the consequent need to consider the vulnerability of dispersed units and the possibility of fleet actions. War is an option of difficulties, but it can be argued that ministers, generals and admirals were guilty of a failure of judgement in the light of the information and resources available to them. Opportunities were missed, and they were worth grasping at the expense of other objectives.

The royal governors of the southern and middle colonies had little to turn to in 1775 to preserve their authority apart from a few warships. The potential for action was indicated by Lord Dunmore, the Governor of Virginia, who, with two warships, two companies of regulars from St. Augustine and some armed Loyalists and Negroes, seized the towns of Gosport and Norfolk. Virginia had a smaller percentage of active Loyalists than other states, but there were many in and near Norfolk, and, supported as he was, Dunmore was able to win their assistance. He issued a proclamation emancipating slaves who joined his force and launched a number of raids before being defeated at Great Bridge on 9 December 1775 and obliged to move his force afloat.[21] Admiral Graves and General Gage argued that they could not provide any support for Dunmore, althought the amphibious force that destroyed Falmouth would probably have been better employed helping Dunmore and sustaining a second front in Virginia. Due to desertion and expiring enlistments, Howe's force soon outnumbered the Americans beseiging Boston and there was no question of an American naval blockade of that port.

On the other hand, American success in intercepting British supply ships discouraged the dispersal of British warships.

Other governors argued that they could have done more had they been provided with support. Given the substantial reinforcements sent to Boston, it is worth noting the claim of Robert Eden, the Governor of Maryland, that one regiment would have quashed resistance there, or the pressure from Josiah Martin of North Carolina for assistance. The possibilities that amphibious power offered were indicated in Rhode Island and Georgia. The threat of naval gunfire allowed the British to use Newport as a naval base until the squadron was withdrawn in March 1776, while, after attempts to purchase rice at Savannah for the Boston garrison had failed, a night raid there that month led to the seizure of 18 merchantmen carrying rice.

British generals and admirals did not like to disperse their strength, amphibious operations were difficult to execute successfully and units that would have been landed might have found it difficult to obtain supplies and might have risked defeat at the hands of larger American forces, the retreat from Concord being repeated up and down the eastern seaboard. In adition, the naval strenth in American waters before the late spring of 1776, and usually even after that, was possibly insufficient for the task of supporting Loyalists sufficiently to give them much confidence. It is not difficult, however, to feel that the specific character of the war at this stage, as an armed struggle in which it was crucial to seize the local initiative in order to inspire Loyalism and while Britain's opponents were poorly-organised and trained, was not properly grasped by British leaders who were unduely cautious in the after-effects of Bunker Hill. A British pamphlet of 1776 complained that the Americans had been given 'the advantage of gaining time to form a union of counsels, to adjust plans of action, to turn their resources into the most convenient channels, to train their men in regular discipline, and to draw to their camp ammunition and stores, and all the necessary implements of war'.[22]

Arguably the same problems that were to face the British in the south in 1780-1 would have affected earlier operations there: to make a sufficiently widespread impact it would have been necessary to dispatch substantial forces and thus the British army in America could have been defeated in detail. On the other hand, aside from the fact that dispersed British forces in fortified positions could repel attack, as at Quebec in 1775 and Savannah, Stono Ferry and Castine in 1779, the Revolutionary position in 1775-6 was far less consolidated than it was to become, while British control of the sea was not challenged effectively until French entry into the war in 1778. It is not difficult to feel that opportunities were missed and that the British failed to make adequate use of their sea power. The easy capture of Newport in December 1776 and of Savannah in December 1778 suggests what could have been achieved earlier. It should have been possible to capture ports in the middle and southern colonies, even if a major force had not been sent to operate in the interior. Indeed a 'southern strategy' offered both these alternatives, and the eventual failure of the attempt to control the interior does not invalidate the alternative of garrisoning crucial ports, a policy that was dependent on naval power. In addition, British posts at Savannah and Charleston would not have had to confront the main American army. Indeed, once captured by the British, in 1778 and 1780 respectively, they were not to be lost until the British withdrew at the end of the war. A Franco-American attack on Newport was repelled successfully in 1778, and the port was abandoned in 1779 as part of a regrouping of forces, not because of American pressure.

If it is argued that the linchpin of American resistance was Washington's army then an advocacy of dispersal may seem valid, but beside the point. The greatest failure of the Royal Navy can then be seen as the failure to cut off Washington's retreat from Brooklyn after the battle of Long Island, and possibly even across the Delaware in December 1776, an option Howe rejected in favour of securing Newport. America, even during the Revolutionary War, was a continental power and the same strategic lessons about the limits of naval power applied to America as they did to France and Russia. In other words, a maritime power such as Britain, could raid, blockade, send fleets, and even occupy strategic points, such as New York and Charleston, but the issue could not be decided unless an army could be put ashore which could conquer the land itself. This is what happened to the South during the American Civil War and to Germany in 1945. Fleets with small armies could not achieve this. The problem in the Revolutionary War was to get the Americans to consent to rule by London. Any policy or strategy which did not destroy Washington's army and conquer the country, forcing consent on the Americans, arguably would not have worked. In this analysis, fleets, raiding, blockades, and the burning and occupying of cities could not have achieved this end.

Reluctant to send troops to the south, Sir William Howe, commander in chief in North America 1775–8, was also unwilling to heed the idea of amphibious attacks on New England, the only means left that the British had to strike at this centre of disaffection. In early 1778 Lord George Germain, Secretary of State for American affairs, instructed Howe to attack the New England ports, in order to destroy their warships and privateers, and thus hit American trade. This would not only complement the British blockade, but might also help to counteract criticism in Britain about the failure to prevent American privateering. Howe replied:

> Your Lordship is pleased to direct that these troops should be detached consistent with the defensive plan I have proposed ... to send a considerable force from hence does not appear to me advisable; considering that the remainder would not be able so far to improve any successful operation in the field, or other favourable circumstances that may occur, as to change the defensive into an offensive plan, which I presume is an idea that an army, though acting on the defensive, should always entertain... less than 4,000 would be insufficient for the proposed service, being fully persuaded a smaller number making a descent on the coast of New England, where there may be an object in view, would very soon be opposed by a great superiority of force ... and the difficult navigation upon these coasts, with a fleet, the frequent fogs that prevail, the want of a convenient port of rendezvous, the flatness of a great part of the coast, which must impede the receiving of necessary assistances from the shipping, as well in landing, as in the reimbarkation of the troops, will, I fear, render any effectual service extremely hazardous.[23]

There was considerable force in these observations, but Howe's reply was inadequate. Successful attacks were mounted, as against Danbury in 1777, New Bedford in 1778 and the Chesapeake, New Haven, Fairfield and Norwalk in 1779. The War of 1812–15 was to show what was possible with a rather strong naval force on the American coast.

French entry into the war altered the parameters of amphibious operations. Instead of simply considering the American military and political response, it was necessary to face the prospect of a loss of maritime superiority. France's entry led to a redeployment of British naval resources, as Britain responded to the integration of the American conflict into a wider struggle, in which the naval balance in American waters was interrelated with that in European and, more obviously, Caribbean waters. Thus, the war ceased to be exceptional in maritime terms.

The arrival of the French in American waters—d'Estaing was spotted by the British off the entrance to the Chesapeake on 5 July 1778—reflected the failure to keep the French fleet in European waters. The desirability of blockading French ports, and thus of preventing the French from intervening in America or the West Indies, pressed by Germain, clashed with the argument, strongly advanced by the Earl of Sandwich, First Lord of the Admiralty, that British naval strength should be concentrated in defence of home waters. Such a course entailed keeping a close eye on Brest, but, by failing to blockade Toulon or block the Straits of Gibraltar, the Toulon fleet would be left free to sail to North

America (and British trade in the Mediterranean would suffer). If the French made such an attempt a matching squadron could theoretically be sent in pursuit, although it was possible that the French fleet might inflict serious damage before the British arrived. A fierce governmental dispute over strategy[24], exacerbated by concern over the general level of British naval preparedness, which swiftly became a political issue, was not eased by naval success. There was to be no famous triumph until Rodney's victory at the battle of the Saints in 1782. Proposing in March 1779 a motion of censure on the government for not sending sufficient ships to Admiral Lord Howe at New York the previous year, Charles James Fox, the leader of the opposition in the House of Commons and a former Lord of the Admiralty, claimed that:

> ...if Lord Howe had been reinforced, or the Streights of Gibraltar watched, in either event the effect would be similar; that of securing to Lord Howe the full advantage of the force under his command, or giving him a superiority in case the Toulon squadron was permitted to cross the ocean.

The failure to blockade Toulon was also bad for British prestige. It looked back to Byng's debacle off Minorea in 1756 and to the British refusal to act over the French acquisition of Corsica in 1768 and thus contrasted with the more assertive stance of British naval power in the Mediterranean between 1693 and 1748. In 1778 the British Consul in Nice, then a possession of the King of Sardinia, wrote:

> I long for the appearance of our squadron in these seas, could you not inform me when it may be expected to quiet a little the storys set on foot by the French emissarys, that we have neither money nor allies and that our ships dare not stir out of our ports.[25]

Admiral Keppel failed, however, to destroy the outnumbered and evasive Brest fleet off Ushant on 27 July 1778, a crucial failure in terms of the balance between British naval commitments in home and trans-oceanic waters. Thirty ships of the line were engaged on each side in the battle. Had the French been defeated prior to the Spanish entry into the war the following year, the British position would have been far stronger; indeed the Spanish might have been deterred fron acting.

The naval campaign of 1778 was also a failure for France. France's one moment of near parity with Britain in naval strength came at the beginning of hostilities, as Britain took longer to mobilise her naval resources, because she was dependent on taking sailors from arriving merchantmen. D'Estaing, who had sailed from Toulon on 11 April, was able to reach American waters. The British were vulnerable in three respects. First, their forces were based on ports, New York and Newport, or islands in the Caribbean, and if these were cut off from maritime supplies they might well be forced to surrender, as Lord Howe was to point out in Parliament.[26] Secondly, army movements were by water, and in 1778 a number of important moves had to be made, both short distance in the case of the last stage of Clinton's retreat from Philadelphia to New York, and long range: the projected detachments thence for St. Lucia, the Floridas and, eventually, Georgia. D'Estaing tried to intercept the St Lucia expedition in late 1778. The following year, Admiral Byron argued that French naval superiority in the Caribbean made it foolish to attempt to move Grant's force back from St Lucia to New York. Thirdly, if a superior French fleet defeated a smaller British one, it would alter not only the balance of naval advantage in American waters, but also the Anglo-French maritime balance of power, with possibly fatal consequences for the defence of home waters.

Having threatened New York, but failed to mount an attack, the French struck at Newport in 1778, but abandoned the siege as a result of storm damage. There was no decisive naval engagement. Howe avoided one at New York, a battle off Rhode Island was preempted by a storm and thereafter Howe failed to intercept d'Estaing on his retreat to Boston and refused Clinton's pressure for an amphibious attack on Boston, in order to destory the French fleet. This naval campaign was to be typical of those in American and Caribbean waters in 1778–80. There was to be no decisive naval battle until the Saints. The battle of the Chesapeake on 5 September 1781 gave France tactical control of the Chesapeake and paved the way for Yorktown. The temporary and localized French superiority that it reflected and sustained was not, however, the consequence or cause of a climatic batle in which one fleet destroyed the other and, as a result, it did not lead to a decisive shift in naval superiority.

Similarly, there was no decisive battle in home waters. The Bourbon attempt to invade Britain in 1779 was thwarted by disease and poor organization, rather than by British naval action. The French envoy in London had reported in April 1777 that the British Navy 'est en effet ce qui constitue la principale force de ce pays-ci, si ce n'est même l'unique garant de son existence politique'.[27] It was soon clear that it could not deliver the decisive victory over France that was necessary if other hostile powers were to be prevented from entering the fray or adopting a hostile neutrality. In addition, the loss of West Florida (1781) and Minorca (1782), and the successful build-up of a powerful Franco-American force around Yorktown (1781) revealed that the Bourbons could mount successful amphibious attacks.[28]

On the other hand, the British Navy was still able to mount a formidable challenge, as in the three reliefs of Gibraltar, which enabled that fortress to resist the long siege of 1779–83. This was , however, a major burden on naval resources. Technological advances were also made. Copper sheathing reduced the difficulties caused by barnacles, weeds and the teredo worm, and the consequent loss of speed. A crash programme of coppering, driven forward by Sir Charles Middleton, Comptroller of the Navy 1778–90, began in February 1779 and was completed by 1781. That year, the Marquess of Rockingham claimed:

The *copper bottoms* occasioning our ships to sail so much better enables us either *to go and attack* if we should see an inferior fleet or *to decline* the attempt if we should see a superior fleet.

The value of copper sheathing in the conduct of naval operations has recently been queried, but the administrative achievement was considerable. Another development was the introduction of the carronade, a new short-barrelled gun that was very effective at close quarters. It was used with effect at the Saints.[29] Indeed, British vitality so impressed the French foreign minister that he wrote in February 1783:

J'ai peine encore à concevoir, Monsieur, ce qui a pu déterminer le ministère britannique aux sacrifices énormes que lui coûte cette paix. Tous ses moyens, à la finance près, sont supérieurs à ce qu'ils étaient avant la guerre. Sa marine est plus nombreuse et mieux constituée.[30]

Given British maritime strength, it is easy to appreciate the arguments of those who pressed for peace with America, so that an offensive war with the Bourbons could be pursued. This was the argument not only of the opposition, but also of ministerial figures who sought compromise with America. Prior to Yorktown, the diplomat Lord Mountstuart expressed his hope that such a peace could be negotiated, but none with the Bourbons 'as long as they have 80 ships of the line to oppose to us'. Spanish America appeared vulnerable to attack.[31]

The Peace of Versailles of 1783 did not end Anglo-Bourbon tension. Indeed, the vigour of French activity in Indian waters at the end of the war under the dynamic command of Suffren helped to exacerbate British concern that France would seek to deprive Britain of India as she had of America. The argument of John Trevor, envoy in Turin, in 1786 that 'we cannot keep too strict an eye upon every motion of the French in the East Indies', was commonplace. Thomas, Lord Walsingham, a member of the Board of Control for India, wrote to Pitt in 1786, 'The Governor General says 2 French frigates could stop all supplies and all communication with Madras, and he adds, the worst of consequences will follow unless you have a naval force on a rupture equal to your enemies.' This concern helped to explain British anxiety about closer Franco-Dutch relations in 1783–7, as in Cape Town and Ceylon the Dutch had crucial bases on the route to India, which complemented those of France in Mauritius and Réunion. George Rose, an MP who was joint-secretary to the Treasury and a confidant of Pitt's, wrote to William Wilberforce, a fellow-member of Pitt's circle, 'The struggle is whether this country or France shall have the assistance of Holland in future contests; I do not scruple to say that almost our existence both at home and in the East Indies depend upon that.' The French Navy continued strong after 1783, with 61 ships of the line on 1 January 1787 and 65 on 1 January 1793.[32] The British envoy in The Hague, Sir James Harris, wrote of 'France, whose object is to form a mass of maritime power against us'. The development of a new harbour at Cherbourg created considerable concern.[33] The press devoted a lot of attention to French naval activity and helped to incite concern. On 3 January 1785, the *Daily Universal Register* commented on a report that Spain was constructing warships, 'All this is said to be done at the instance of the French, who leave no means untried to make the naval force of the House of Bourbon equal, if possible, to all the other powers of Europe'. The same paper reflected on growing Bourbon naval strength on 27 July 1786, 'the consequences of this conduct must in the end change the name of Great Britain into that of Little England', adding on 25 August 1786:

> ...situated as France is at present with all the powers around her, in the strictest alliance with or dependence upon her, except Britain, she has nothing to dread from a continental war; and if she can acquire a decided superiority of naval strength, which, considering her revenue, is far from impossible; especially if she considerably diminishes her force by land, she may with care deprive us of our distant possessions one after another, and when that fall, our fate is not far distant. No expence therefore ought to be thought too great for our Navy, on which, as we stand alone in Europe, our very existence as a nation must depend.

The ousting of the pro-French 'Patriot' government in the Dutch crisis of 1787 helped to alter the naval balance in Britain's favour. The Anglo-Dutch naval relationship had become a less important one and the Dutch increasingly seemed less impressive as a naval power. Trevor wrote in 1783 of 'the little exertion they made during the late war'. The Dutch role, however, was measured less in the number of their ships able to sail, than in bases and strategic situation. In addition, given the fact that British naval inferiority off the Virginia Capes in September 1781 was a matter only of a few ships, the impact of Dutch entry into the War of American Independence on the Bourbon side in terms of the additional commitment for the British home fleet cannot be discounted. The Dutch prepared 14 ships of the line in 1781, 19 in 1782, and opened the North Sea as a new theatre of war. Pitt argued that the importance of the United Provinces included, 'from the maritime strength which it might at least be made capable of exerting (when acting under the direction of France who would naturally turn everything to that object)'.[34]

The British were thus assured of Dutch support after 1787. Initially, it still seemed likely that any war would be with France, and sensitivity over the Indian Ocean remained strong. The Chevalier de la Luzerne, sent to London as French ambassador in January 1788, sought, without success, to reassure the British, and fears did not ease until the breakdown of order in France with the Revolution.[35] In fact, although war was indeed to break out with France, this was not until 1793, and the naval confrontations of the intervening years were staged not with France, but with first Spain and then Russia. From late 1787 France was already clearly weakening as a naval power, a consequence of the increasing financial problems of the government. This, as much as any shift in diplomatic alignments, helped to give the British a greater margin of relative naval power. In August 1788 the French envoy argued that the British Navy had never been so formidable, and that this obliged France to improve hers, but she was unable to do so. Arthur Young noted that month that the work at Cherbourg had stopped. In the spring of 1789 domestic circumstances prevented France from fulfilling plans to send a squadron of observation to sea that would manoeuvre jointly with that of Spain. The Spanish first minister, Count Floridablanca, was very disappointed, as he had hoped that the planned joint manoeuvres would impress the rest of Europe. Montmorin, the French foreign minister, expressed the hope that it would be possible to stage joint manoeuvres in 1790[36], but in fact the failure of 1789 prefigured that of 1790 when France failed to provide adequate naval support to Spain in her naval confrontation with Britain.

The seizure in 1790 by Spanish warships of fur-trading British vessels trading on Vancouver Island, part of the extensive American territories Spain claimed, rapidly escalated towards war. On 12 April Anthony Merry, the Consul in Madrid, reported thet twelve ships of the line at Cartagena were to be prepared for sea. Three days later he added that fourteen of the line, ten frigates, and two sloops were to be fitted out for immediate service at Cadiz. Count Floridablance, the leading Spanish minister, however, assured Merry on 17 April that these naval preparations were designed not against Britain, but in response to the danger of a revolt in the Spanish colonies in the West Indies inspired by French sedition. Merry accepted this assurance, and repeated it on 29 April, when he reported that 24 ships of the line were preparing in Spain, adding 'the quickness observed in arming here is much greater than it was expected the Spaniards would have been capable of'. Robert Walpole reported from Lisbon on 28 April 'some late letters from Madrid say, that thirty ships of the line, besides frigates are ordered to be got ready.'[37] The British, in turn, prepared a large naval force. By early May Floridablance was no longer claiming that the armament was designed for the West Indies. The Earl of Fife expressed the general attitude, 'I always think the best way to secure peace is to have our Navy on a respectable footing'. He also saw Spain's diplomatic position as crucial:

> I do not see the least prospect they have for support from any other power, from the present state of other kingdoms; and it is very hard when this kingdom was in so glorious a way of getting out of all difficultys to go to war for a rabbit or other's skin—I have no ambition for extended dominions but only to manage what we have.[38]

Clearly the French attitude was vital. It was argued in Spain that Britain would not have dared to confront her but for French weakness.[39] The Third Family Compact was still in force and France was obliged to come to Spain's assistance, but the French government, faced with a deteriorating domestic situation, initially sought to offer conciliation.[40] The French were suspicious of British intentions. Indeed two contradictory assumptions were a persistent theme in Anglo-Bourbon maritime rivalry. The British felt that their naval preparedness and actions were a response to Bourbon threats, whether in the Turks and Caicos Islands, Honduras and the Gambia in 1764–5, over the Falklands in 1770, or over Nootka Sound. Conversely the Bourbon attitude that British naval strength was cause and consequence of the destruction or absence of any oceanic balance of power, and that Britain was determined to use her strength in order to destroy rival trans-oceanic empires was widely held in Europe. These fears were exacerbated by French weakness from 1787, which seemed to end any hopes of a maritime balance. In May 1790 the French envoy in Vienna expressed his fears that Britain would exploit French weakness in order to attack Spain and that such an attack would be mounted only in order to later attack France.[41]

Although the Spaniards said that they could find other allies 'upon the failure of France'[42], the British had more success in this respect. Their Prussian ally was in no position to help, and although Walpole was instructed to find out if the Portuguese government would let British warships into Lisbon, Portugal was exposed to Spanish pressure.[43] The Dutch, however, sent a squadron under Van Kinsbergen to join the British warships assembling at Spithead. Auckland praised their 'most becoming and efficient activity',[44] and the Dutch position vindicated the attitude of those who had seen the fate of the United Provinces as so crucial in 1780–7. The Dutch role has been treated as largely inconsequential[45], but this is largely the perspective of hindsight. Had the French fulfilled their promise to come to Spain's assistance in 1790 or had the confrontation reached the state of armed conflict, then Dutch assistance might well have been valuable and it would anyway have been a factor in the arithmetic of relative naval strength that played such an important part in naval and political attitudes towards commitments, deployment and operations.

The British fleet that was prepared in 1790 was a considerable one, benefitting from post-war expenditure. Pitt and Middleton had adopted a costly peace-time plan to revitalise the Navy, at least in warships. Both saw a strong Navy as the sine qua non of a strong foreign policy. This notion had long enjoyed support, but Pitt was willing to pay to make it a reality.

On 3 May 1790 the Admiralty was ordered to assemble 40 of the line as quickly as possible at Spithead. Auckland felt that one benefit of the crisis was that it had 'shown to Europe that we are able in the course of a few weeks to produce a fleet such as perhaps the united efforts of Europe cannot match'.[46] On 18 August 31 of the line and 17 other ships sailed from Torbay. In contrast, 26 of the line and 10 other ships left Cadiz on 20 July 1790. The Spaniards sought French assistance. In May the French ministry had ordered the preparation of 14 of the line, but on 26 August the National Assembly voted to provide 45 such ships. Montmorin pointed out that there were only 30 ships, and there was general scepticism about France's ability to fulfil her promise. George Rose, however, observed:

> ...the French can neither man or pay a fleet, nor would the municipalities allow provisions to go out of the provinces to victual one; in addition to which I am assured not an officer of credit will serve in a squadron where there is and must be a total want of discipline; and yet I fear the mischief as to encouraging Spain is nearly as great as if these difficulties did not exist.[47]

Rose was drawing attention to the vital role of perception in naval power. Fleet actions involving most of the battle-worthy capital ships of combatant powers were not a commonplace feature of naval conflict in the eighteenth century and overwhelming victories were unusual. There were examples, such as Cape Passaro in 1718 and Chesmé in 1770, but indecisive battles, such as Toulon (1744), Ushant (1778) and Virginia Capes (the Chesapeake, 1781) were more common. Tactically indecisive battles could of course be strategically decisive. This was true of Virginia Capes, arguably in that sense the greatest French victory in the age of sail. Though battles could be successful as a means of providing a test of naval primacy, they obviously could not fulfil such a function in peacetime, and yet then questions of relative naval power played a major role in diplomatic calculations.

This was to be demonstrated abundantly in 1790–1. Without any conflict, British naval power triumphed in the former year and yet was rebuffed in 1791. The British triumph in 1790 owed much to the *perception* of naval power. The Spanish sense that they could not rely on France's ability to fulfil their promises of naval preparedness[48] played a major role in their decision to settle with Britain, whle the fact that the British had the same view encouraged them to persevere. The British decision not to embark on a war of conquest was also important, for most British commentators were convinced that they would triumph if war broke out. Rose observed 'the Spaniards are mad, for they must lose their colonies by a war without our moving much', while Robert Liston, an experienced diplomat, was encouraged by the possibility that the north west passage ran from near Nootka Sound to Hudson's Bay and that there was a large inland sea, such as the Baltic or Mediterranean. He added:

...if the coasts of this new Mediterranean are of a rich sort, producing ship-timber, and peopled with a race of men wishing to exchange furs for our woolens and manufactures, we cannot give up such an extensive prospect for the increase of our trade.

The 3rd Duke of Richmond, Master-General of the Ordnance and an influential member of the Cabinet, sent Pitt an important letter about Caribbean possibilities:

I think with you that the force you mention having in the West Indies, viz. 6,000 disposable troops very ample for taking Trinidad, and for another expedition to New Orleans, and I do not think there is any other object that presents such a probability of success. The Havana, Hispaniola, and Porto Rico appear to me to be too great undertakings at first. As any operation that requiresa a regular siege is destruction in the West Indies, and great loss of men in the beginning of the war would cramp all our future operations. Trinidad and New Orleans seem to require but few men, and perhaps Buenos Aires might also be carried with the force you mention. There are no other alternatives that I know of except the places on the north side of South America such as Caracas, Porto Bello, Carthagena etc. but it seems to me that they should not be undertaken till Trinidad is in our possession which gives us a good port to windward and a communication with the continent from whence we may get intelligence and perhaps assistance from the inhabitants, giving them arms to revolt ... although an attack on Trinidad appears to me very easy and I think one on New

Orleans, may be attended with the most important consequences, yet both require great judgement in the execution and particularly that on New Orleans, both in the execution and in the planning, for it is distant from all our other possessions in America and so much to Leeward, that unless it is well combined with other operations, with those of the fleet, and with a knowledge of the force and dispositions of the enemy, all we send there may be cut off, and become another Burgoyne business.[49]

Richmond's observation is interesting in light of the fate of the British expedition to New Orleans during the war of 1812. Such ideas were echoed in the press. A London report in the *Gloucester Journal* of 18 October 1790 declared, 'The West Indies will be the grand theatre of action, and there we have everything to hope, and our enemies to dread. A superior force we shall certainly have in those seas; and, for our dependencies, they are in a far better state of security than those belonging to any other power.' 'Britannicus', writing in the *Public Advertiser* of 1 November 1790, pressed the need to act against Spain, called for bold action and made reference to Drake and Elizabeth I. There was a general sense of naval confidence. The same paper, in its issue of 6 November, announced:

The preparations in the dockyards of France, have produced only 14 ships of the line: Every Englishman must exult in the comparative difference— We have nearly as many three-decked ships at Spithead at this moment; and besides the squadron which sailed under Amiral Cornish, a fleet of forty-six ships of the line, ready for immediate service.

Bellicose sentiments were voiced widely, but, however aggressive British policy might appear to other governments, a striking feature of the crisis was that it was *not* used as an opportunity to attack the Spanish empire. As in 1770 over the Falklands, British policy was reactive. In 1790 the Spanish empire was seen as weak and unstable, France was unable to come to her assistance and the British Navy was at a high standard of preparedness. The opportunity for deploying Britain's potential as maritime power had possibly never been greater.

And yet there was no war, and moreover, a settlement, signed on 28 October 1790, that was not a complete abdication of the Spanish position.[50] This was due not only to the basic pacific intentions of the British government, intentions that were particularly well developed in the ministry of the Younger Pitt, with his strong sense of economy, but also to that most crucial parameter of naval power, Britain's diplomatic position. In 1790 Britain was involved in complex negotiations designed to end the war in the Balkans, that had begun in 1787, on the basis of the *status quo ante bellum*. Austria, weakened by internal discontent, had been persuaded to accept these terms, but Russia, under Catherine II (the Great), was determined to preserve some Balkan conquests. Britain's ally, Frederick William II of Prussia, keen to weaken Austria and Russia, and at least to prevent them from gaining territory, was ready to use the threat of force in order to obtain this end.

It was not, therefore, desirable for Britain to become involved in a naval conflict with Spain at a time when the rest of Europe was in a volatile situation. The notion of conquering 'America' while France or 'Germany' were taken care of, not by diversionary British and British-subsidised troops, but by internal rivalries, had no appeal to British policy-makers. Instead, in the second half of 1790 the idea developed of using the naval power that had been mobilised against Spain in order to give force to the intimidation of Russia.

The apparent need for such a commitment and the weight that was placed upon it steadily increased. Discussing the projected Anglo-Prussian 'concern of measures', Francis Jackson wrote in August 1790:

> All that is required here is that Russia may not be allowed to employ her naval force against the coasts of Prussia, and that a declaration should be made at Petersburgh to that purport, and supported, *if necessary*, by the appearance of a fleet in the Baltic; of this, however, the necessity appears very doubtful; as the very idea of such an apparition will probably suffice to frighten the Russians into almost any terms that may accompany it.

The following month Joseph Ewart, who, as envoy in Berlin, had been instrumental in committing Britain to a more interventionist policy in eastern Europe, wrote:

> I think a great deal might be done this season yet by overawing, through the vigour of our demonstrations and remonstrances, as I cannot conceive that the Empress of Russia can be so mad as to wait the execution of our threats next year.

Ewart proposed that 30 ships of the line sail from Torbay to the Downs, whence they could more easily sail to the Baltic, and he subsequently returned to his theme that Russia would be affected if a fleet assembled in the Downs.[51]

At the end of the Nootka crisis, 32 ships of the line and 12 frigates were kept in commission, and Lord Hood was given command of the proposed Baltic fleet. The government also considered sending a squadron to the Black Sea. Among the over-optimistic assumptions about the potential of naval action that circulated was that of the Swedish envoy in London who told his French counterpart that the British could send 15 warships to destroy the Russian Black Sea fleet and cut communications between the Crimea and the southern Ukraine, allegedly a very easy task, so that, with the aid of the troops from the fleet, the Turks could overrun the Crimea.[52]

There were, however, serious questions about the practicality of British action. The Russians might choose, as in the crisis at the end of the Great Northern War, not to engage in a naval action with the British. The possibility of effective economic warfare was queried:

> Should the Empress not give way, and our fleet enter the Baltic, it will probably meet nothing but French vessels laden with the productions of Russia, which by our treaty with France we cannot molest... what mischief will our fleet be able to do to Russia? at most to burn the poor port of Revel, after which, ice will force us from those seas into our ports.[53]

Thus, while the British prepared 'one of the finest English fleets that ever went to sea', a fleet that was scrutinised with care by foreign governments[54], there was growing concern about its likely military effectiveness. As a continental power without a trans-oceanic colonial empire, Russia was not vulnerable to the disturbing threat of a naval power, and there were no plausible targets for amphibious action. It was not, however, military factors that were to lead to the decision not to employ the Navy. Domestic agitation, which in part reflected the activity of the Russian envoy Simon Vorontsov and the opposition's sense of an opportunity to defeat the ministry[55], exacerbated divisions within the cabinet and the diplomatic corps and was reflected in a falling majority in the Commons. Arguably as important was the deteriorating international situation. Sweden had abandoned her war with Russia, there was uncertainty over Austria's position and Prussian policy was quixotically unstable. The situation was not propitious for war, no more than it had been in 1720–1 at the end of the Great Northern War.[56]

Pitt's misguided sense that the political nation would support confrontation with Russia, and the government's failure until too late to appreciate the weakness of its diplomatic position, forced it into a humiliating climbdown in the spring of 1791, but part of the problem was an erroneous assessment of national power in the aftermath of the Dutch and Nootka Sound crises. The *World* of 1 April 1791 claimed that, albeit with Algerine and Dutch support, the British would be able to defeat the fleets of Spain, Russia and Sweden. One observer suggested:

> The young gentleman's easy victory over the cats of Nootka Sound, seems to have induced a propensity for continuing to play with the feline genius; but if I am not much mistaken the old Russian tabby will scratch him harder than he expects.[57]

The role of naval power had been central in all British confrontations with other powers since 1763. In addition, the successful outcome of the Seven Years' War (1756–63) had suggested that deficiencies as a land power could be compensated for by maritime success. British policy makers were not old enough to remember a different strategic world. George III had been born in 1738, his Foreign Secretary, the 5th Duke of Leeds in 1751, William Pitt the younger in 1759. They had to re-learn the two crucial strategic lessons of the first half of the century, both of which focussed on the limitations of naval power. The first was that such power was of limited value against a continental power. This had been learned in the Great Northern War and was demonstrated anew in the Ochakov Crisis. It was not so much a question of the deficiencies of the Navy in any war against such a power, because war was only the last option. Naval power was most effective in international relations when it was used to intimidate and threaten, not to fight, but continental powers could not be treated thus, because they were not all in the same situation.

The second lesson was that of 1745–8, that maritime success had to be assessed against failure on the European mainland. In 1748 Britain had been forced to return her strategic gain of Cape Breton in order to ensure a French withdrawal from the Low Countries. In the French Revolutionary and Napoleonic Wars, Britain was to learn that maritime and oceanic gains could not prevent the French from dominating Western Europe with all the strategic and economic dangers that that posed, and by the Peace of Amiens of 1802 Britain returned her colonial conquests to France. Such classic 'blue water' sentiments as those expressed by Alexander Thomson in 1798 were misleading:

> While the known valour of our country bids defiance to their menaces, and the vigilance of administration continues to guard us from the danger of improvident security, we may reasonably hope still to preserve our national independence, and to compensate the preponderancy of power on the Continent by asserting the empire of the ocean.[58]

The period 1775–91 highlighted some of the problems of British naval power, but the absence of war in western Europe ensured that the full extent of the strategic dilemma that would face Britain in a major war was not grasped. Logistics and the problems of mounting amphibious operations had ensured that only a relatively small French expeditionary force had been sent to America and, although it was to play a crucial role at Yorktown, it did not pose a military threat to the British comparable to the substantial armies of Revolutionary France. Without an effective Navy, these armies could still destroy Britain's alliance systems, even if a successful invasion of the British Isles eluded them.

The Franco-Austrian alliance helped to keep western Europe peaceful and thus to insulate Britain from the dilemma of seeking to reconcile interests in continental Europe with a military capability that was more dominated by a Navy than that of any other European power. Though the alliance of 1756 might seem largely empty of meaning after 1763, with French opposition to the Austrian acquisition of Bavaria or the opening of the Scheldt, it kept the peace in the Low Countries and the Rhineland, and thus solved what had been a central problem for British foreign policy since 1677: how best to respond to French expansionism on the Continent. This problem and Britain's strategic dilemma was posed from 1792 in an increasingly acute form, forcing new directions in foreign, strategic and military policy as Britain faced a crisis that was unprecedented in the experience of its governers.

ACKNOWLEDGMENTS

I would like to thank the British Academy and the Staff Travel and Research Fund of Durham University for assisting my research, and Jonathan Dull for discussing the Anglo-French aspect of the War of American Independence with me.

NOTES

1. *Four Letters to the Earl of Carlisle* (2nd ed., London, 1779), 53; J.G. Droysen et al., ed., *Politische Correspondenz Friedrichs des Grossen* (46 vols., Berlin, 1879–1939), 46, 538.
2. P. Mackesy, *The War for America, 1775–1783* (London, 1964); D. Syrett, *The Royal Navy in American Waters 1775–1783* (Aldershot, 1989); J.M. Black, *War for America. The Fight for Independence 1775–1783* (Stroud, 1991); A.T. Patterson, *The Other Armada. The Franco-Spanish Attempt to invade Britain in 1779* (Manchester, 1960). Syrett produced a first-rate review in his 'American and British Naval Historians and the American Revolutionary War, 1875–1980', *American Neptune*, 42 (1982), 179–92.
3. J. Dull, *The French Navy and American Independence: a study of Arms and Diplomacy 1774–1787* (Princeton, 1975), 312–17, 233–4; D. Baugh, 'Why did Britain lose command of the sea during the war for America?', in J.M. Black and P.L. Woodfine, eds., *The British Navy and the Use of Naval Power in the Eighteenth Century* (Leicester, 1988), 152–63.
4. P.L.C. Webb, 'The rebuilding and repair of the fleet, 1783–93', *Bulletin of the Institute of Historical Research*, 50 (1977), 194–209; R. Morriss, *The*

Royal Dockyards during the Revolutionary and Napoleonic Wars (Leicester, 1983), 13.

5. L. Marinas Otero, 'El Incidente de Nutka', Revista de Indias, 27 (1967), 335–407; Webb, 'The naval aspects of the Nootka Sound crisis', The Mariner's Mirror, 61 (1975), 133–54.

6. P.L.C. Webb, 'Sea Power in the Ochakov Affair of 1791', International History Review, 2 (1980), 13–33. The best introduction to the Navy and foreign policy in this period is Webb, 'The Navy and British Foreign Policy, 1783–93' (M. Litt, thesis, Cambridge, 1971).

7. Dull, 'Mahan, Sea Power, and the War for American Independence', International History Review, 10 (1988), 65; W. Cobbett, Parliamentary History of England from ... 1066 to ... 1803 (36 vols., London, 1806–20), XXV, 1001–2; J.P. Merino Navarro, La Armada Espanola en el Siglo XVIII (Madrid 1981); J.D. Habron, Trafalgar and the Spanish Navy (London, 1988); R.D. Bourland, 'Maurepas and his administration of the French Navy on the eve of the War of the Austrian Succession' (Ph.D. thesis, Notre Dame, 1978); Black, Anglo-Spanish Naval Relations in the Eighteenth Century', Mariner's Mirror, 77 (1991) 235–58.

8. Black, 'The British Navy and British Foreign Policy in the First Half of the Eighteenth Century', in Black and K.W. Schweizer, eds., Essays in European history in honour of Ragnhild Hatton (Lennoville, 1985), 137–55; J.B. Hattendorf, 'Admiral Sir George Byng and the Cape Passaro Incident, 1718 : A case study in the use of the Royal Navy as a deterrent', in Guerres et Paix 1660–1815 (Vincennes, 1987), 19–38.

9. G. Modelski and W.R. Thompson, Seapower in Global Politics 1494–1993 (London, 1988), 231, 260, 280.

10. H.M. Scott, 'The Importance of Bourbon Naval Reconstruction to the Strategy of Choiseul after the Seven Years' War', International History Review, 1 (1979), 28, 35.

11. N. Tracy, Navies, Deterrence, and American Independence. Britain and Seapower in the 1760s and 1770s (Vancouver, 1988), 42–55.

12. G. Lacour-Gayet, La marine militaire de la France sous le règne de Louis XV (2nd ed., Paris, 1910), 412–28; J.S. Pritchard, Louis XV's Navy 1748–1762 (Kingston, Ontario, 1987).

13. N. Tracy, 'The Falkland Islands Crisis of 1770: Use of Naval Force', English Historical Review, 90 (1975), 40–75; Tracy, Navies, 69–99.

14. R. Harding, Amphibious Warfare in the Eighteenth Century. The British Expedition to the West Indies, 1740–1742 (Woodbridge, 1991).

15. J. Gwyn, 'The Royal Navy in North America, 1712–1776', in Black and Woodfine, eds., British Navy, 144–5; D. Syrett, 'Defeat at Sea: The Impact of American Naval Operations upon the British, 1775–1778', in Maritime Dimensions of the American Revolution (Washington, 1977); Syrett, Royal Navy, 26–7.

16. C.W. Stephenson, 'The supply of gunpowder in 1776', American Historical Review, 30 (1925), 271–81; E.S. Kite, 'The Continental Congress and France: Secret Aid and the Alliance 1776–1777', Records of the American Catholic Historical Society of Philadelphia, 39 (1928); Kite, 'French "Secret Aid". Precursor to the French Alliance, 1776–1777', French American Review 1, (1948).

17. W.B. Clark, *George Washington's Navy* (Baton Rouge, Louisiana, 1960); W.M. Fowler, *Rebels under Sail: The American Navy during the Revolution* (New York, 1976); J. Dull, 'Was the Continental Navy a mistake?', *American Neptune*, 44 (1984).
18. J.R. McNeil, *Atlantic Empires of France and Spain: Louisburg and Havana, 1770–1763* (Chapel Hill, 1985).
19. W.H. Whiteley, 'The British Navy and the siege of Quebec, 1775–6', *Canadian Historical Review*, 61 (1980).
20. Nottingham University Library, Clumber papers 2342, 2321; E. Robson, 'The expedition to the southern colonies, 1775–1776', *English Historical Review*, 66 (1951).
21. W.H. Moomaw, 'The British leave colonial Virginia', *Virginia Magazine of History and Biography*, 66 (1958); A.J. Mapp, 'The "Pirate" Peer: Lord Dunmore's Operations in the Chesapeake Bay', in E.M. Eller, ed., *Chesapeake Bay in the American Revolution* (Centreville, 1981).
22. *Reflections on the Present State of the American War* (London, 1776), 5.
23. London, P[ublic] R[ecord] O[ffice], PRO 30/55/8, 10.Germain to Howe, 18 Feb. 1778, Howe to Germain, 19 April 1778.
24. G.S. Brown, 'The Anglo-French Crisis, 1778: a study of conflict in the North Cabinet', *William and Mary Quarterly* (1956); D. Syrett, 'Home Waters or America? The dilemma of British naval strategy in 1778', *Mariner's Mirror*, 77 (1991), 365–77; I.D. Gruber, *The Howe Brothers and the American Revolution* (New York, 1972), 281–5.
25. W. Cobbett, *Parliamentary History*, XX, 332; Manchester, John Ryland Library, Eng. Mss. No. 1145, Birkbeck to Poyntz, 13 May 1778.
26. Dull, 'Mahan', 62; Cobbett, XX, 340–1.
27. Paris, Ministère des Affaires Étrangères, Correspondance Politique Angleterre (hereafter AE.CP.Ang) 522, f.491, Duke de Noailles to Count de Vergennes, French foreign minister, 25 April 1777.
28. N.0. Rush, *The Battle of Pensacola* (Tallahassee, 1966); C. Fernandez-Shaw, 'Participation de la Armada Espanola en la Guerra de la Independencia de Los Estados Unidors', *Revista de Historia Naval*, 3 (1985), 75–80; D. Gregory, *Minorca, The Illusory Prize. A History of the British Occupations of Minorca between 1708 and 1802* (London, 1990), 187–93.
29. Sheffield City Library, Wentworth Woodhouse Mss. R1–1962, Rockingham to Earl of Hardwicke, c. April 1781, ; J.E. Talbott, 'Copper, Salt, and the Worm', *Naval History*, 3 (1989), 53; Talbott, 'The rise and fall of the carronade', *History Today*, 39/8 (1989), 24–30.
30. AE.CP. Espagne 610 f.223, Vergennes to Montmorin, envoy in Spain, 9 Feb. 1783, quoted in *Guerre d'Amérique et Liberté des Mers 1783–93* (Paris exhibition catalogue, 1983), 68.
31. London, British Library, Department of Manuscripts, Additional Manuscripts (hereafter, BL, Add.MS) 36,803, ff. 78–9, Mountstuart to Murray, 2 June 1781; Add.MS 35,527, f.163, Alexander Straton to Robert Murray Keith, envoy in Vienna.
32. PRO, F[oreign] O[ffice] 67/5, Trevor to Marquis of Carmarthen, Foreign Secretary, 8 April 1786; Cambridge University Library, Add. MSS 6958, Walsinghem to Pitt, 16 July 1786; Oxford, Bodleian Library MS. Wilberforce d 17/1, f.19, Rose to Wilberforce, 27 Sept. 1787; Dull, *French Navy*,

398; Dull, 'Why did the French Revolutionary Navy Fail?', *Consortium on Revolutionary Europe. Proceedings for 1989* (2 vols., Athens, Georgia 1990) II, 125.

33. BL, Add.MS 35,536, ff.106–7, Harris to Keith, 28 Feb. 1786; AE.CP. Ang 557, f.45, Barthélemy, French envoy in London, to Vergennes, 18 July 1786; *Daily Universal Register*, 27 Sept. 1786; *Felix Farley's Bristol Journal*, 6 Jan. 1787; Black, 'The Marquis of Carmarthen and relations with France 1784–1787', *Francia*, 12 (1984), 291–2.
34. PRO, FO 62/3, f.290, Trevor to Charles James Fox, Foreign Secretary, 17 Dec. 1783; Dull, 'Mahan', 64; C. Ross, ed., *Correspondence of Charles, 1st Marquis of Cornwallis* (3vols, London, 1859), I, 321; Paris, Archives Nationales, Archives de la Marine, B7 454, Marianne, agent in Rotterdam, to Luzerne, 31 Mar.1788; N.A.M. Rodger, 'The British View of the Functioning of the Anglo-Dutch Alliance, 1688–1795' is fuller and more accurate than E.S. van Eyck van Heslinga, 'A Competitive Ally. The Delicate Balance of Naval Alliance and Maritime Competition between Great Britain and the Dutch Republic, 1674–1795', both in G.J.A. Raven and N.A.M. Rodger, eds., *Navies and Armies. The Anglo-Dutch Relationship in War and Peace 1688–1988* (Edinburgh, 1990). Neither has much to say about the 1780s.
35. Black, 'Anglo-French Relations in the Age of the French Revolution 1787–1793', *Francia*, 15 (1987), 415–16.
36. AE.CP. Ang. 566 f.137, Barthélemy to Montmorin, 9 Aug.1787, Espagne 626, ff.241, 267, Montmorin to Lemarchand, chargé d'affaires in Madrid, 24 Mar., Lemarchand to Montmorin, 6 April 1789; A. Young, *Travels during the years 1787, 1788 and 1789*, (2nd ed., 2 vols, London, 1794) I, 94–6.
37. PRO, FO 72/16 ff.256, 261, 270, 294–5, Merry to the Duke of Leeds. Foreign Secretary, 12, 15, 19, 29 April 1790; FO 63/13, Walpole to Leeds, 28 April 1790. His despatch of 26 May included details of Spanish preparations transmitted by the Portuguese government; Joseph Brame, Consul at Genoa, to Keith, 18 May, Green, Consul at Nice, to Keith, 20 May 1790, BL, Add.MS 35,542, ff.181,185.
38. PRO, FO 72/17, f.3, Merry to Leeds, 3 May 1790; Aberdeen, University Library, Tayler papers, 2226/131/816, 817, 819, Fife to his factor, William Rose, 5, 7, 22 May 1790; PRO, FO 72/16, f.238, Merry to Leeds, 29 Mar. 1790.
39. Oxford, Bodleian Library, Bland Burges papers vol. 30, f.23, Lord Auckland, envoy at The Hague, to James Bland Burges, Under Secretary, 18 May 1790; AE.CP. Espagne 629, f.112, Puyabry, envoy in Madrid, to Montmorin, 7 July 1790.
40. PRO, FO 72/17, ff.52–3, Alleyne Fitzherbert, newly appointed envoy to Spain, reporting discussions with Montmorin, to Leeds, 15 May 1790; AE.CP. Ang. 573, f.116, Montmorin to Luzerne, envoy in London, 17 May 1790; AE.CP. Autriche 359, f.256, Montmorin to Noailles, envoy in Vienna, 5 May 1790.
41. AE.CP. Autriche 359, f.285–6, Noailles to Montmorin, 22 May 1790. The same report circulated in Parisian newspaper and in diplomatic circles later in the year, Francis Drake, envoy in Copenhagen, to Burges, Bland Burges 34, f.1.

42. PRO, FO 63/13, Walpole to Leeds, 20 June 1790.
43. PRO, FO 63/13, Leeds to Walpole, June 1790.
44. BL, Add.MS 35,542, f.254, 34,433, f.1, Auckland to Keith, 15 June, Auckland to Leeds, 1 Sept. 1790. The French envoy Caillard reported that if Britain sent a fleet to the Baltic, the Dutch would also send ships, Caillard to Montmorin, 19 Aug. 791, AE.CP. Hollande 581, f.75.
45. Rodger, 'British View', 26–7.
46. Bod.Lib., Bland Burges 30, f.47, Auckland to Burges, 11 Aug. 1790.
47. PRO, FO 95/7, ff.330, 381, 391–4, Reports on Spanish naval preparations, 13, 16, 26 June 1790; AE.CP. Espagne 629, f.231–2, Montmorin to Puyabry, 1 Sept. 1790; BL, Add.MS 34,433, ff.23, 159, Speigel to Auckland, 1 Sept., Rose to Auckland, 24 Sept. 1790; PRO, FO 72/17, f.53, Fitzherbert to Leeds, 15 May 1790.
48. AE.CP. Espagne 629, f.355, Puyabry to Montmorin, 26 Oct. 1790.
49. BL, Add.MS 34,433, ff.27, 117, Rose to Auckland, 2 Sept., Liston to Auckland, 14 Sept. 1790; Cambridge University Library, Add. Mss. 6958, no.857, Richmond to Pitt, 16 Oct. 1790.
50. New Haven, Beinecke Library, Osborn Shelves C 114, Dr. Charles Blagen to Lord Palmerston, 22 Nov. 1790; J. Ehrman, *The Younger Pitt. The Years of Acclaim* (London, 1969), 568.
51. Bod. Lib., Bland Burges 36, f.60, Jackson to Burges, 4 Aug. 1790; BL, Add. MS 34,433, ff.19, 118, Ewart to Auckland, 1, 15 Sept. 1790, Add.MS 34,430, f.17, Jackson to Eden, 1 Jan.1790.
52. Webb, 'Sea Power in the Ochakov Affair', 22; AE.CP. Ang. 577 ff.147–8, Luzerne to Montmorin, 15 April 1791.
53. Anon., *Serious Enquiries into the Motives and Consequences of our present armament against Russia*, (London, 1791) 58–9.
54. BL, Add.MS 46,822, f.170, Auckland to Drake, 5 April 1791; AE. Mémoires et Documents, Angleterre 2, ff.119–42, Etat général des forces maritimes de l'Angleterre.
55. A. Cunningham, 'The Oczakov debate', *Middle Eastern Studies*, 1 (1964–5).
56. Black, *A System of Ambition? British Foreign Policy 1660–1793* (London, 1991), 245–6.
57. Preston, Lancashire Record Office, Cavendish of Holker MSS. DD Ca 22/19/2, Dr. Campbell to My Lord, 31 March 1791.
58. A. Thomson, *Letters of a Traveller on the Various Countries of Europe, Asia, and Africa* (London, 1798), 152.

7

SIR GEORGE COCKBURN AND THE MANAGEMENT OF THE ROYAL NAVY, 1841-6

Roger Morriss

Sir George Cockburn was first naval lord at the Admiralty under Lord Haddington and Lord Ellenborough between September 1841 and July 1846. The period is interesting in the history of the Navy because it was central in the transition from sail to steam. Between 1841 and 1846 the sailing fleet declined from 345 to 282 vessels (a decline of 18 per cent), while steam vessels rose from 48 to 71 vessels (an increase of 48 per cent).[1] It saw the first fears of invasion since 1815, with the crisis in relations with the French in 1844 and the realization that steam could rapidly bridge the Channel. This in turn revived concerns to replace impressment by a practical alternative for more rapid mobilization, and to reduce the preponderance of elderly men at senior levels in the officer corps. Steam and the threat of invasion thus resulted in the re-examination of a range of contentious issues, bringing professional and popular, Whig and Tory views into perspective.

In this Cockburn was important because as a professional officer he had a view on policy in almost all areas of naval management, and as a tory first naval lord he had influence both in goverment and on public opinion in the House of Commons. Moreover his importance was not confined to the period 1841 to 1846. It is probably fair to say, indeed, that he had had more influence at high level on the administration of the Navy than any other single professional officer since 1818 when he first joined the Board of Admiralty. In considering the personalities that most influenced the nature of the Navy in the first half of the nineteenth century, it is consequently necessary to focus on Cockburn as one of them. An examination of his views must therefore help to explain why the Navy had reached those stages in development it had by the mid 1840's. Cockburn was unquestionably a very able naval man, probably the most able of his generation.[2] He had played important parts in the Napoleonic Wars and War of 1812 with the United States, as well as in post-war administration. His best known war-time roles were to accompany the army that burned Washington in 1814, having been the rear-admiral commanding in the Chesapeake; and to take Napoleon to St Helena where he was the first governor of the island before the arrival of Sir Hudson Lowe. Between 1818 and 1827 he was second naval lord—but certainly the most outstanding of the Admiralty commissioners. Between 1827 and 1828 he was councillor to the Duke of Clarence, then the last Lord High Admiral; it was Cockburn's stand against the Duke that forced the latter to give up the office. Between 1828 and 1830 he was first naval lord and in 1832 he was sent by the Whigs (though he was a Tory) to be commander-in-chief on the North American station where he remained until 1836. By that time, he had seen almost continuous service since his entry in the Navy in 1786.

One of the problems that exists in examining Cockburn's influence between 1841 and 1846 is the necessity continually to contend with pre-judgements about him and naval administration at that time. For the character Cockburn has been given—in particular by Sir John Briggs in his Naval *Administrations 1827 to 1892* has been transferred by historians and the reading public to naval administration as a whole in the period. Looking back over half a century of technological progress, Briggs depicted Cockburn as the archetypal reactionary:

> In his capacity he was the most uncompromising representative of things as they were. He seemed to live in the past, and was impressed with the conviction that everything that had been done was right, that what was being done was questionable, and every step in advance was fraught with danger.

According to Briggs, 'almost every opinion he expressed, every measure he devised, and every step he took, were retrograde in their tendencies'.[3] It is therefore necessary continually to consider whether Cockburn was the reactionary Briggs depicted, and whether he really did resist change in the Navy, even before one can assess his actual influence. It is intended here to begin this process of reassessment and to suggest the nature of the influence he now appears to have possessed.

In considering his potential influence, it would be wrong to set out with exaggerated expectations. In September 1841 Cockburn was 69 and there is no question that the following five years were a severe strain on him. In addition he encountered serious administrative difficulties which, especially before 1844, hampered and frustrated him. The first of these problems was the weight of work on him personally. He took overall responsibility for dockyards and for shipbuilding, for the selection of vessels for particular services, providing advice on their officering, and took a principal part in the preparation of naval estimates. Apart from letter, order and minute writing in his own office, there were also board meetings and occasional debates in parliament touching the Navy in which he had to participate.

A concomitant problem lay in his own devotion to these duties. He was in modern parlance a workaholic. He admitted he found the work 'constant drudgery' from which there was 'very little relaxation' that 'made it a great sacrifice of all other social enjoyments'. His release from office in 1846 thus made him feel 'like a boy leaving school for the holidays'.⁴ Yet he was avaricious in his application. In 1845, Lord Haddington, the first lord, observed that if Cockburn continued at the Admiralty, 'It would be well ... to force the dockyard[s] from him and [he] have the usual business of his position only—but it would be like taking a bone from a hungry mastiff'.⁵

Aggravating these two problems was the arrangement of Admiralty responsibilities. In 1832 the Navy and Victualling Boards had been abolished, their business being transferred to the charge of five principal officers at Somerset House. Each principal officer was accountable to a superintending Admiralty commissioner: that is, the principal officers performed the greater portion of the real management, while the Admiralty commissioner took the responsibility and issued the orders for his line of business. However the business of both Admiralty commissioners and principal officers grew steadily between 1835 and 1845. For example, the number of officers' appointments grew from 1,736 to 2,701; letters received at the Admiralty rose from 26,973 to 39,275; while dockyard employees grew from 7,884 to 12,194 men.⁶ Time for the principal officer to report and discuss business, and for the Admiralty commissioner to assert control and be really responsible tended to decline in proportion, leading to a sense of loss of control.

Combined with this was a problem of horizontal communication between the Admiralty commissioners themselves, even though they regularly sat as a board. Cockburn summarised his opinions on the operation of the Board of Admiralty after leaving office. It was, he claimed:

...most inconsistent and inconvenient that one member of the board should, without any communication with his colleagues, issue orders at Somerset House, in the name of the board, for the governance of the whole fleet, dockyards, &c., provided it relates to the branch of the Admiralty business he is selected to superintend, such orders being issued in the name and under the authority of the board, without any other member thereof being aware of such order, and often only learning its promulgation from the newspapers, or from questions asked about it in Parliament ... The board [could therefore remain] wholly ignorant ... of such general orders, or of the grounds thereof, unless the particular lord of the department mentions the matter to his colleagues, which, in the latter part of my being at the board, was very rarely done, especially by one of my colleagues; consequently the business could not but be carried forward in an unconnected and disjointed manner,...[7]

There was too a problem of communication with a civilian first lord. There is no doubt Cockburn put himself out to keep his superior well briefed. Indeed before taking office Haddington had been somewhat alarmed at the prospect of working with Cockburn, although Melville had tried to reassure him. But in March 1842, after six months' experience, Haddington had to admit how right Melville had been. Haddington found Cockburn 'invaluable'. It was 'perfectly impossible for two men... to go on better than we do'. He had seldom known a man he liked better. His frankness assisted him, his confidence reassured him, 'and his bluntness and occasional buntades [sic]' he cared 'not a chaw about'.[8] But for Cockburn it was a burden to have a first lord whose ignorance of naval matters had continually to be accommodated. This very ignorance encouraged Haddington to concentrate on his political role within the Cabinet. But, as a result, he left almost all purely naval matters to Cockburn, who nonetheless had to keep him informed. In his strictures on the Board of Admiralty, Cockburn later pointed out that nothing could be more contrary to reason and common sense 'than for a person to be selected to preside at such professional board, who is totally unable and admits his inability to understand three-fourths of the professional statements or even expressions contained in the various documents read on such occasions to the board, and which, therefore, the professional members of the board become obliged to occupy time in explaining...'[9]

Yet it was in debate at the board that Cockburn met his most serious problems. Until 1846 meetings were held on alternate days, and attended by as many commissioners as were available and by the first or second Secretary. As the most experienced professional officer, the first naval lord generally proposed how a letter should be answered, when the others either agreed or differed as they saw fit.[10] But like other earlier critics of board management, Cockburn frequently encountered opposition and found the board more of an impediment than an aid to business:[11]

... the board, consisting of six persons, and the professional members, or a portion of them, being selected with reference to political considerations and their having seats in Parliament, and without any regard to their knowledge of each other or how far they might be likely to act cordially

together, much valuable time becomes consumed in fruitless and sometimes irritable and unsatisfactory discussions, interfering greatly with the
necessary advancement of the numerous professional and other matters
almost daily brought for decision before the Admiralty ...[12]

It would be wrong to attribute all the administrative difficulties
encountered at the Admiralty to the system of individual responsibility
and the political incompatibility of the commissioners. Cockburn's own
personality seems also to have generated hostility. He could assume, as
Briggs recalled from their first meeting, 'a very imperious and very
overbearing' tone though one that was replaced, after the ice was broken,
'with the greatest politeness and kindness'.[13] An apparent arrogance or
haughtiness was evidently adopted with all those that he wanted to keep
at a distance. Sir George Seymour, his principal office opponent for two
and a half years, was answered soon after he joined the Admiralty,
having proposed changes in captain's pay structure: 'Sir George will
learn 'ere he has been much longer at the board that however specious
in theory that suggestion may be ...'![14] Experienced, knowledgeable,
precise and determined, Cockburn's expertise and authority must have
been difficult to manage, especially from a junior situation. Capping
Cockburn's competence was a lucidity on administrative matters that
defied contradiction. His rough minutes were full, expository, logical and
easy to read. They bespoke a command of Admiralty administration that,
while helpful to Haddington, was no doubt stifling to a man like Seymour.

It has been suggested that Cockburn managed these difficulties by
ruthlessly dominating the board.[15] Certainly his experience, ability and
personality permitted him to manage in the face of these difficulties. Yet
written evidence calls into question his supposed ruthlessness. He
appears to have had too much respect for the niceties of constitutional
practice actually to set out to dominate the board. His conclusion to a
long minute on the service of naval officers in the Coast Guard aptly
reflected his attitude: 'Having thus freely stated my impressions on the
whole subject, whatever Lord Haddington and the majority of my colleagues deem to be the best course to be adopted under the existing
circumstances ... I shall not hesitate to accede to, feeling that the points
I have submitted will have received due and impartial consideration and
that the decision of the majority is the most likely to prove right on the
whole.'[16] Such readiness to accede to the opinions of others did not come
easily with the length of his experience and general strength of his views.
Nevertheless he did concede points, concessions which J.H. Briggs, then
the reader to the board, later depicted with malicious pleasure:

He [Cockburn] argued ... with an ability it was difficult to gainsay. Still he found it at times almost impossible to resist the strong representations made to him by Mr Herbert [first or 'political Secretary'] and Mr Corry [civil commissioner]. It was very amusing to see one on one side and one on the other rather persuading and coaxing rather than arguing the question. Yet you could perceive he was gradually giving way and conceding the point against his will and professional judgement.[17]

However to Cockburn the management of the Navy appeared to suffer from the opposition he encountered. He himself had causes to advance.[18] But with the 'want of concert' at the board, he recalled 'frequent annoying checks and obstructions in carrying forward those objects which appeared to him essentially required and called for, and some of which I was obliged to abandon from the opposition of one or other of such disjointed ruling body'.[19] Undoubtedly Cockburn's deepest distress arose from the opposition of two professional colleagues, Sir George Seymour and Captain William Gordon. Supported by Haddington's private secretary, Captain Baillie Hamilton, and by the civilians Corry and Herbert, these two officers had the odds on their side.[20] Cockburn was supported by Vice Admiral Sir William Gage. But board meetings were evidently an ordeal. 'Unworthy jealousies', annoyances and debates kept him 'in a continual state of anxiety and difficulty' and required from him 'the strongest exertion of forbearance' to enable him 'to remain in a situation so truly unsatisfactory' to his view of efficient management.[21]

The situation was helped no doubt by the retirement from the board of Sir George Seymour in May 1844. But the strain involved in overcoming these difficulties took its toll first on Cockburn. In January 1843 he suffered from what was described as the 'rupture of a blood vessel in a lung'. Owing to his 'importance as a public figure', Prince Albert was advised for the information of the Queen.[22] Attended by Dr. Alexander Nisbet, naval surgeon at the Royal Hospital, Greenwich, he was to appearances restored to health by March 1843. Cockburn himself acknowledged that the illness had been dangerous, and for some months even his private correspondence was suspended. That summer a continental holiday was necessary and that winter of 1843–44 he was advised to avoid attendance in the House of Commons whenever possible, advice he followed until after Easter. Early in 1844 he felt uncommonly well, and a holiday that autumn gave him a few days' relaxation. Yet by mid–1845 he was again labouring under his burdens, keenly looking forward to the end of the parliamentary session, 'my work in the office all day and in the House of Commons all night being almost too much for anybody'.[23] By then Cockburn was 73, and still to perform another year of duty.

There can be no doubt that these difficulties drained Cockburn of some of the energy which he might have exerted in managing the Navy. Yet here it must also be acknowledged that the scope possessed by a first naval lord to influence the shape or nature of the Navy was less than might be expected. For the ships that were commissioned, and those ordered to be built for the Navy, were largely decided by two factors beyond the control of even the first lord.

The most important of these factors was the supply of finance. Between 1841 and 1846 the number of men voted for the Navy fell overall by 9 per cent. In the short term between 1842 and 1844 the number of men voted fell by 21 per cent. This in turn reduced the number of ships that could be commissioned from 257 to 225, a reduction of 12 per cent. It was only limited to that by an increase in the number of smaller vessels at the cost of larger ones. In 1844, out of the 225 vessels commissioned, there were only 27 larger than sixth rates.[24]

How this large number of small vessels and few rated ships was used was principally determined by the second factor—the demands for ships for foreign and home stations. 'Growth' stations in this period were the East Indies and China station, owing to the China War and the Nanking Treaty agreement of 1842; off the coasts of Africa where anti-slave trade patrols were increasing; and off South America. To meet these demands the numbers of ship in the Mediterranean, off North America, and in the West Indies shrank. But there were also demands for duties like the packet service and surveying and of course for ships on the home station for defence.[25]

Between the numbers supplied by finance and those in demand there was little scope for indulging preferences in ships commissioned. Perhaps this is why Briggs emphasised Cockburn's inclination to maintain many hulks and obsolete vessels in Ordinary or reserve.[26] Certainly, he believed 'a certain strength of line of battle ships fit for service of paramount importance' considering them 'far more powerful in fact, as well as in the effect on the minds of foreigners, than razées or other frigates'. But he was 'by no means disposed to disparage' the offensive power of heavy 4th rate frigates that were more economical to commission than ships of the line.[27] Even so, the cost of commissioning these was still relatively high. Thus the crisis with the French in 1844, and Palmerston's warning in 1845 that steam power had created a 'steam bridge, to land 30,000 troops on the south coast overnight, led to the equipment of only one more ship of the line and two more 4th rate frigates by 1846.[28]

Given this limited capacity to enlarge the Navy even for defence, it is understandable why the choice of ships to build or commission should be contentious. For each choice carried differences in firepower and manning, the arguments for and against which were matters of opinion. Within the Admiralty arguments were put to paper as well as voiced at the board. From a long minute answering the observations of Sir George Seymour about 1843, we know Cockburn had very firm opinions but was equally explicit in setting them forth for his colleagues to consider.[29]

Ironically, in view of Briggs comments, among the Admiralty commissioners the extension of the steam Navy does not seem to have been a matter so contentious as the choice of sailing ships to commission. Briggs tells us that:

> Sir George was, both politically as well as professionally greatly opposed...
> to the introduction of steam, and on one occasion went so far as to declare
> that since the introduction of steam-vessels he had never seen a clean deck
> or a captain who, when he waited upon him, did not look like a sweep.[30]

This was quoted by Geoffrey Penn in *Up Funnel, Down Screw! the story of the naval engineer*(1955) who had the impression that Cockburn was opposed to steam throughout the whole of his career.[31] Briggs was in fact referring to Cockburn in the period 1828–30, when he was previously first naval lord. Yet against Briggs' recollection, in this case spanning 60 years, should be set a letter written in September 1830 to John Wilson Croker, the Admiralty Secretary, by Cockburn from Walmer clearly expressing his exhilaration at sailing under steam, and acknowledging its speed and ability to defy the elements:

> We have a magnificent surf here today and a good deal of sea outside. I
> have sent Lightning & Confiance to proof their powers against it. Confiance
> came 60 miles with us yesterday, as far or nearly so as Lightning. In the
> latter part of the day she fell astern... and was twelve minutes behind us
> in letting go her anchor here. We both beat Echo quite wonderfully. We had
> fine weather and smooth water all the way and were just nine hours from
> Deptford to Walmer.[32]

As first naval lord between 1841 and 1846, Cockburn's management of the steam fleet in no way suggests a discontinuance of his appreciation of its capabilities. Under Cockburn the steam fleet grew from 48 to 71 vessels, a rate of growth of 4.6 vessels a year. This rate compares favourably with the growth for the larger 15 year period, 1835 to 1850, when the steam fleet grew from 20 to 76 vessels at a rate of 3.7 vessels a year. These periods mask short-term bursts of growth. But examining even these, that over which Cockburn presided was quite comparable with others before and after. Between 1838 and 1841 the fleet had grown from 21 to 48 at a rate of 9 vessels a year. Under Cockburn an increase from 54 to 71 vessels between 1844 and 1846 was at a rate of 8.5 vessels a year. Between 1846 and 1847 there was a remarkable addition of 15 vessels in one year. However it seems likely that at least some of these vessels were acquired as a result of orders placed under Cockburn.[33]

Even though the steam fleet grew markedly, it should not be forgotten that at the beginning of Cockburn's administration in 1841 the steam fleet still numbered only 48 vessels, while sail numbered 345 vessels. Moreover sail still carried the main armament of the fleet. Steam undoubtedly held out its promise, but sail could not be dispensed with. Each of course had its own advocates and projectors, while Cockburn had the task of attempting to further improvements in both. What did he achieve?

In sailing ship design he attempted to further the nascent science of naval architecture. To Cockburn's mind the problem was 'to get an exact principle, and have nothing further to do than determine size'. Proposals for improvements were still repeatedly being heard at the Admiralty. There were too many to refer all to Symonds, the Surveyor appointed by the Whigs in 1832. At the same time Symonds was thought not to be the most impartial of judges. In 1845 Cockburn claimed he 'was free to say that he did not think his ships were perfect and he knew that when persons took up a system they sometimes became too exclusively attached to it; so it was felt right that some check should be kept on that valuable officer'.[34] That check, instituted in 1841, soon after Haddington's board came into office, was a committee of dockyard master shipwrights sitting at Woolwich. In March 1842 Cockburn had declared how:

... he hoped the result of their deliberations would be to obtain the best possible mode of building ships, and also how to place as many guns as could be fought consistently with strength, not forgetting the more important points of sailing against head seas and off lee shores.[35]

Significantly Symonds' vessels were known neither for their capabilities against head winds nor for their stability as gun platforms. The recommendations of the Woolwich committee were nevertheless referred to Symonds and most were adopted, though 'modified to a certain extent by the Surveyor's observations'.

The Board of Admiralty next selected three of the most able graduates of the former Portsmouth school of naval architecture, abolished in 1832, 'to meet as a committee to examine scientifically the errors of construction of our former system of building'. The graduates were also commissioned to 'submit to the Admiralty the lines they would propose for a ship of each class as the most perfect according to the principles their science should dictate'.[36] This committee's immediate product was the *Espiegle* brig, which in the autumn of 1844 was put on trial with seven other experimental brigs. For the theoreticians the results were disappointing. Croker, the former Admiralty Secretary, gave his impression of them in February 1845:

> I am quite aware of the results (as they are called) of the late trial of the brigs, having read what the papers have given of the reports;—but if I had not read a word, I should have been nearly as well informed, for the reports are just of the same vague and unsatisfactory kind that every report that I ever remember now near 40 years has been. One is better on a wind, another better, pie [*sic*]:- one stows better but slow; another fast but cannot stow, one beats everything, but she also beats herself by carrying away her own masts and spars, and so ad infinitum, and the result is a kind of algebraic equation of various qualities really incommensurable and coming to no absolute and intelligible standard of merit.[37]

There were other trials of brigs and battleships in 1844 and a 'grand trial of line of battleships of each class' in 1845.

However in March 1845 Cockburn admitted the difficulty of finding 'any exact principle which could be said to be really best'. In November 1845 he thus took up the idea of a 'scientific board of construction' subordinate to the Admiralty:

> It is in my opinion quite clear [he wrote to Haddington] that with the rapid advance science is making in every other branch of profession, the naval service ought to have the full benefit of this spirit, and that naval construction ought to be formed on more fixed and certain principles. I therefore submit for consideration the propriety of establishing a supervising board of construction to which the Admiralty may refer for detailed explanations in favour of or against the lines or draughts of all ships or steam vessels hereafter built ...[38]

Haddington supported the idea; so did Ellenborough his successor and so did Peel. This 'committee of reference' was established in 1846 and examined all designs including those of Symonds who was to resign in 1847.[39]

Cockburn oversaw other things in aid of naval architecture. In particular to replace the Portsmouth school abolished by the Whigs in 1832, dockyard schools for the instruction of shipwright apprentices were established in 1844. In June 1846 Cockburn claimed that the Admiralty 'had done everything' possible 'to obtain every scientific information on the subject of the design of vessels'.[40] In view of the existing state of knowledge and the previous absence of official information-gathering organs, this was a claim that carries credibility.

Cockburn must certainly be given credit for recognising the need for education in ship design. For he was fully aware of this necessity in the development of steam ships. He pointed out in 1845: 'it was not to be supposed that former Boards of Admiralty should at once have learned by inspiration to make perfect steamers: but, unless they had built the boats they had built, the present board would not have known how to improve the building as they would not have had the opportunity of finding out the defects of previous constructions'.[41] Cockburn also encouraged others like Sir Charles Napier and the Earl of Dundonald to submit drafts for steamers.

Cockburn's own contribution was to increase the size and to reduce the power-weight ratio of the ships being built. 'One of the first things that struck me on my return to office', Cockburn wrote to Peel in September 1842, 'was the want of power and efficiency of the steam ships of the Navy, to remedy which evil the surveyor of the Navy has been ordered to build a steam ship of war of much larger dimensions than any hitherto constructed in our dockyards, and engines have already been ordered to be prepared for her of double the power of any we have hitherto used'. Proposed for royal use and launched in 1843, this vessel probably became the royal yacht *Victoria and Albert* of 1,442 tons and 400 horse power.[42] As with *Victoria and Albert*, so with other vessels. Particularly on account of the increase in engine size, across the complement of steamships, the power to weight ratio of the Navy declined dramatically from almost 1:5 to 1:3, where it was to remain for the remainder of the decade.[43]

In retrospect, because paddle steamers could only be armed with bow and stern guns of long range, some like the shipwright officer John Fincham were to question the value of building larger steamships. Larger vessels were more expensive to build and maintain, but carried guns of a size equally well carried by smaller vessels. Given similar power to weight ratios, moreover, smaller vessels may have been able to move as quickly as larger ones. However, other factors affecting speed— engine weight, location and efficiency, as well as hull form—were also under trial, and at the time the only sure way of realising the actual effect of varying any aspect of design was to try it in actual construction.[44]

In consequence the design and equipment of steam vessels was still a very hit and miss affair. Their draught seems to have been unpredictable, preventing them carrying the armament or the number of troops expected. Sir Charles Napier was particularly virulent in his attacks on Admiralty construction, denying for example in May 1845 'that any material improvements had been made ... since the *Gorgon* and *Cyclops* were built ten years ago'. He claimed that the steam Navy was 'unfit for war purposes' an opinion that was deeply challenging in view of the deterioration in relations with the French.[45]

What was Cockburn's view? He made no absolute claims. But he thought that British steamships were more fit for war purposes than the French, in particular their latest products. He claimed that the French steamers of 450 horse power resulting from their 1840 ocean-going packet programme were underpowered.[46] 'Considering their large size and draft of water .... it will afford to our ships so much greater power in proportion to their size, a most important superiority, by placing it in the power of ours to choose their position for attack, to close or to retreat as may be most desirable under the circumstances in which they discover the enemy's vessels'.[47]

This in turn made him sanguine about the threat of war. With a greater number of superior steamers and with sufficient ships of the line 'in advanced state for commissioning', there was no reason for Britain to fear a French invasion. His one anxiety attached to the degree of dispersal of the British steam fleet. This gave rise to weakness in the Channel, 'for as fast as we get steam vessels of war fit for service they are called for some pressing duty abroad and we are obliged to detach them'. He therefore recommended they 'keep determinedly a certain number of these steam vessels for duty at home, the Admiralty to be authorised not to furnish them for any distant duty without special directions from the Cabinet'.[48]

The improvement in naval steamship building which has attracted most attention lately has been the introduction of the screw propeller. In 1958 it was suggested that 'the tedious and repetitious lag between invention and general adoption' was 'particularly evident in the slow transition from the paddle-wheel to the screw-propeller'. Recently D.K. Brown and Andrew Lambert have revised our view of that transition and shown that the Admiralty possessed clear aims; that its development of an acceptable screw ship was rapid after an initial wrong turning; and that Admiralty commitment to the project was important to the rapid resolution of the technical problems.[49]

Cockburn evidently shared these aims. Briefly stated these were the production of an auxiliary screw warship that stowed its propulsive machinery largely below the water-line and left the sides of vessels clear for the carriage of a full broadside. He was certainly involved in the hiatus in proceedings following the change of ministry of 1841 that brought in the Haddington board. Economy seems to have decided the Admiralty to transfer the screw experimentation from the future *Rattler* to the existing sloop *Acheron*, a change at which Isambard Kingdom

Brunel, the 'mechanical director', protested. This protest achieved its object and the choice of vessel reverted to the *Rattler* early in 1842. These changes—though providing a poor impression to Brunel—in fact occasioned only 5 weeks delay, so that the *Rattler* was launched in April 1843, and had her first trial run on 30 October: only 20 months after the reversion in favour of the *Rattler*. But it was the experimentation with 32 different propellers between February 1844 and January 1845 that is most convincing of Admiralty commitment. In view of the costs involved it was a series of trials that probably only the Admiralty could have afforded to make. At the same time other developments were taking place: in particular the trial of a tubular boiler which reduced the weight and space of the steam generating equipment.[50] In all this Cockburn seems to have acted as a coordinator holding the ring between the surveyor, the steam department and Brunel, endorsing recommendations, authorising action, even to the detail of trials of pressure acting upon a safety-valve.[51] He was fully informed of what was being done, and commanded a position that gave control over the whole procedure.

He certainly had hopes for the screw, the progress of which he logged in his speeches in the House of Commons. On 1 March 1844 he declared that 'his impression ... was that they would arrive at the knowledge of a screw which would be better than the paddle-wheels'. In April 1845 the *Rattler* towed the *Alecto* and in May Cockburn went so far as to declare that he 'was in hopes before long to have all the vessels fitted with screw instead of paddles' and that 'they were now building with the view of finding the best construction, and... of placing the machinery below the water mark...'[52] Even after the *Rattler—Alecto* demonstration, some like Sir Charles Napier remained unconvinced of the superiority of the screw. By June 1845, however, Cockburn was quite decided, and, apparently without higher authority, had altered the naval building programme accordingly. At that time, he informed Haddington:

> The proofs we have lately had of the efficiency of the screw as a propeller on board the *Rattler* convince *me*, that it will be in future generally adopted and we are now adapting those building for that description of propeller ... The French I believe have only one or two with screw propellers. We are therefore taking the lead in this important change of getting rid of the cumbersome paddle wheels, and with the advantage that a screw vessel may if required be converted into a paddle vessel but a paddle vessel cannot be converted to a screw vessel without much alteration and expense ...[53]

During 1845 as many as 26 engines were ordered for installation in screw ships. The *Amphion*, the Royal Navy's first screw frigate, with all her machinery and boilers below the water-line, was launched in January 1846. The *Ajax*, the first line of battle ship equipped with the screw, went to sea in September 1846.[54] This was less than six years since *Rattler* had been proposed and less than four and a half years since the beginning of her construction.

In view of the Navy's reputation for conservatism, this period of research and development was remarkably brief. Much more detailed work is required to elicit Cockburn's views at each stage in this project. Yet that part of the story already known certainly confutes his reputation for resistance to change in the Navy. Indeed he may even have been inclined to press ahead with innovation in the Navy perhaps too precipitously. In 1844 he thus began sanctioning the construction of vessels in iron: initially six small steamers for use as tenders, and by mid 1845 the construction of 5 large frigates and 25 gun vessels, packets, tenders and schooners.[55] However the use of iron for larger vessels was then discontinued following demonstration of the damage and splintering caused by gun fire on iron hulls in tests attended by Cockburn at Woolwich. Over the next 15 years iron was used for nothing larger than packets, gun and mortar vessels, while the building under Cockburn was condemned.[56] He was here, perhaps, ahead of his time. Even so, the venture certainly suggests a first naval lord unwilling to allow the Navy to slip behind contemporary technology.

It was the new technology, steampower, bringing fears of a rapid cross-channel invasion, that revived agitation in parliament to improve the conditions of seamen. For manning was rightly regarded as the main obstacle to the rapid mobilisation of a defensive fleet. Reformers divided the problem of manning into those of recruitment and desertion, which they attributed to poor conditions of service—that is, inadequate pay and pensions and the persistence of summary physical punishments— the net result being a need to maintain impressment. Reformers saw the conditions as the cause of the greater problem. In their view, an improvement of the conditions would solve the manning problem.

It was in this area that Cockburn best demonstrated his adhesion to traditional practices, even at the cost of his personal reputation. For Briggs ridiculed Cockburn for his refusal to acknowledge the desirability of abolishing corporal punishment and impressment so as to conform with public opinion. Yet Cockburn saw good reason to maintain most conditions of service as they were, especially as he found other more important causes for desertion and difficulties of recruitment.

He differed least with reformers over pensions which he favoured for shorter periods of service than the 21 years for which they were established in the early 1820's. But as to higher rates of pay, he rejected such proposals, believing that whatever the naval rate the merchant service would always be obliged to pay more, resulting in a leapfrogging of pay rates. Logically, moreover, because of their cost, in the short term higher rates of pay may anyway have reduced the numbers of men that could be employed.[57]

With regard to corporal punishment, Cockburn believed that there was still value in a captain being able to summarily award physical punishment up to 48 lashes without resort to court martial. With the necessity for returns by a captain stating the causes and evidence of an offence, combined with explicit Admiralty disapproval for and frequent inquiry into punishments, he felt there was sufficient deterrence to their award where they could be avoided.[58] He believed, indeed, that most punishments were avoidable, and that it was the root cause for an offence that had to be removed. The means of doing this, he argued, was through the proper supervision of men by their officers. For,

...at least nine times in ten it will be found a ship in which there are the fewest corporal punishments will be in the best order and have on board the best and most efficient officers. For it depends in my opinion in a very main degree on the ability and vigilance with which the officers give their constant personal attention in superintending the general conduct of the men, and the steadiness and temper with which they carry on the several duties with which they are from time to time charged, to prevent such crimes as call for corporal punishment. Whereas when on the contrary officers (I allude particularly to the lieutenants) give but little superintending personal attention to the men, and satisfy themselves with merely giving their orders, looking for the captain to punish all infringements of them, the petty officers and seamen, so left to themselves, are but too apt very negligently to obey the orders so given and to fall into excesses which render a resort to corporal punishment ultimately necessary.

Drunkenness, a major cause of punishments, he regarded as a challenge to the management of officers. He admitted some men were impossible to manage, but thus favoured the discharge of 'hardened refractory characters'.

Desertion occurred, in his view, partly for the same reason as punishments: 'generally speaking the ship in the worst discipline lost the most men'. But likewise, the problem was much checked and kept under by quiet and steady discipline ... and granting the men constant leave to go on shore whenever a fair opportunity for it offers, which last point, though it affords the facility, tends in my opinion more than anything else to check the *desire*'. And here, Cockburn certainly spoke from long experience, for he had practised this principle as far back as the French Revolutionary War. Yet desertion could not be stopped entirely. It was in 'the nature of sailors to incline to change with headstrong inconsideration [of] their existing position'. Even so, this inclination worked in favour of the Navy as well as against it:

For the same restless disposition that causes a seaman to run from a ship of war one year induces him to leave a merchant ship the next year, if not sooner, to join some other ship of war, only entering in the latter by some other name, so that they almost invariably return again to the service, and we are therefore generally enabled to keep up our complements abroad wherever we have any trade.[59]

These views prevented Cockburn from accepting that the recruitment problem could be solved by a reduction of desertion, or corporal punishment, or an improvement in pay and pensions. The recruitment problem was, to Cockburn's mind, an economic problem. The taxpayer got as many seamen as he paid for:

The number of seamen allowed by Parliament would always be kept up. They might educate 40,000 boys if they chose, but then if they found employment and bread for only 20,000 seamen the first number would ultimately dwindle down to the latter. The number that maintenance was provided for would always be had, and would always be retained.[60]

The problem for the Navy arose when it reduced its seamen by 3–4,000 one year, and a few years later wanted them back. It then found that those 3–4,000 seamen had turned to other occupations. Against this Cockburn was content to put up with slow recruitment. For an emergency, therefore, when seamen had to be pulled under compulsion from other employments, he maintained that the right to impress men could not for the time being be abandoned. However, at the same time, Cockburn believed that all seamen receiving naval pensions should automatically be liable to service in an emergency. Accordingly an Admiralty order of August 1844 provided that ex-seamen in the dockyards were liable, and late in 1845 all new entrants to the coastguard were put on the same footing.[61]

For an emergency, a hitherto unexploited resource was the list of 188,000 or more seamen and apprentices registered by the Admiralty registrar of shipping and seamen between 1835 and 1839. Interestingly, the registrar's proposal for a naval reserve in 1844 pointed out that the 1696 registry had failed due to the registration of incompetent men.[62] It was therefore possibly no coincidence that also in 1844, in collaboration with Gladstone at the Board of Trade, Cockburn arranged the introduction of voluntary examinations of competence for masters and mates—their names, and whether they had passed, to be entered in *Lloyds Register* in addition to the seaworthiness of ships.[63] This was achieved by 1846. In 1850 the register office was transferred from the Admiralty to the Board of Trade to look after these records of competency, the names of passed masters and mates subsequently appearing in the

Mercantile Navy List. From that time, the registrar thus had command of the names of qualified men as well as of registered ships, seamen and apprentices. The Royal Naval Reserve Officers Act was passed in 1861, when a certificate of competency became a qualification for a commission. Cockburn's work in establishing examinations thus seems to have formed one of the foundation stones for a balanced reserve of competent as well as of ordinary seamen that in the long term became the practical alternative to impressment.[64]

As Cockburn pointed out, within the Navy the ships with least punishments and desertion were those with officers most competent at superintending their men. Such efficiency of man management was a primary element in what Cockburn would have defined as the professional officer. Other elements that took priority were the possession of 'the spirit required for maintaining his independence and the respect due to our national colours' in the face of provocative or insulting action on the part of a potential enemy.[65] In addition there was, of course, the ability not to misinterpret orders to personal advantage, and the ability to act like a gentleman. The character of being a good steam officer was not, to his mind, a recommendation for a command, which possibly accounts for why the master, surgeon, purser and chaplain all gained wardroom status in 1843 while the engineer officer did not until 1847.[66]

In the selection of officers for appointments Cockburn consequently knew what he was looking for. For this reason it was immaterial to him that the officer corps was still little smaller than it had been in 1814; nearly four-fifths inactive on half-pay; overloaded with aged officers; and with large proportions of each rank not having served afloat for long periods or even in the ranks they held. He thus appears neither to have objected nor contributed to the introduction of a new retirement list in 1845 and 1846, prompted by public opinion as a result of the invasion scare of 1844–5.[67] What mattered to Cockburn was that a small proportion of younger men, adequate in total numbers to demand, were being brought through the ranks and gaining experience; also, that those being selected for this experience were those who were able officers, for service at a lower rank was a criterion for an appointment in the next.

Being concerned with professional ability, he was naturally anxious that political interest should not weigh more heavily in the selection process. Appointments were the prerogative of the first lord. But because Cockburn was expected to defend appointments and promotion in the Commons it seems certain that he was consulted as to professional ability before decisions were taken. Indeed it was one of Cockburn's proposals for reform of the Board of Admiralty that the first lord should be a senior naval officer 'competent to form an independent and impartial opinion' of ability; while the fact that he also wished the first lord not to sit in Parliament was an indication that he was fully aware that political considerations still played their part in appointments, even if usually subordinate to professional ones.[68]

That Cockburn did not hesitate to remind his colleagues of the priority of professional considerations over political ones is revealed in a surviving confidential minute. In 1841, he condemned the Whigs' earlier introduction of promotion for length of service in the Coast Guard, even if without service afloat, as 'most mischievous'. It had 'opened a door to innovations which have been taken advantage of for mere political objects to the manifest injury of the service'.[69] However this is not to say that he shed all party interest on entering office. He made occasional efforts to oblige party political contacts through his service friends, but subsequent to appointment, when he expected the subject to prove himself by taking advantage of favourable circumstances. Thus he wrote in 1842 to Sir Thomas Cochrane, Commander-in-Chief in the East Indies:

> Mr John O Bailey, going out as mate of *Agincourt*, is the son of Mr Joseph Bailey & excellent Conservative member of the House of Commons. If you can put him in the way of distinguishing himself or be otherwise of service to him, I and the party will feel obliged to you.[70]

He was no less obliging in the interest of men who had high social connections. For he still favoured the notion of having some 'men of high rank and influence in the Navy'. But it was even more important for those with connections to possess the ability or length of service that justified an appointment. For the morale of officers as well as efficiency was at stake. This was delicately put in his letter of March 1846 to 'My dear Lady Nicholson':

> I send you the report made to me by the Captain Superintendent of Deptford yard relative to Edward Houndorn, and as I feel certain you would not wish me to do an act of injustice, even to favour a protegé of yours, I am sorry to say I cannot comply with your Ladyship's wishes in his behalf, until he shall have served a sufficient time longer in his present station to afford him reasonable claim for further advancement.[71]

In maintaining professional values in the face of political or private interest, Cockburn can be likened to the highest naval officers in the Admiralty before him: Lords Anson and St Vincent spring to mind.[72] It was during the early 1840s that Cockburn became known 'as the first man in the Navy'. It was a title that was not undeserved for, privately as well as officially, he also imposed the view of the Admiralty on the most senior admirals commanding fleets at sea. It was a role in which his seniority, experience and personality gave him a natural ascendency:

> Our board consider Sir William Parker to have ceased to be commander-in-chief from the day on which he sailed from Trincomalee to England [he advised Sir Thomas Cochrane in December 1844]. I understand he is not satisfied with our decision on this point and talks of taking legal opinion about it. I am however very confident of our being right in the view we have taken of it under the Queens Regulations which he *had* received at the time.[73]

Cockburn's precision, combative nature, and faculty for matters of a legal nature—Briggs recalled how well he could 'dispute a point of law'—were formidable deterrents to any dissenters from the Admiralty point of view.

Because of this ability, because of the arrogant manner he could assume, and because of the stands he took on controversial issues of his day like flogging and impressment, there is no doubt that Cockburn had many opponents and some enemies. Fatigue, illness and pressure of work cannot have helped his public image, even within the Admiralty. At the board responding to whatever arose, he probably made the worst of impressions. The 'occasional buntades' that Haddington cared 'not a chaw about', when Cockburn responded by blocking proposals, must have borne the *appearance* to those who were ideologically opposed of someone reactionary in the extreme.

Yet in fact did he hold up development in the Navy? Here of course it is necessary to look beyond the board at what in the Navy Cockburn was actually responsible for. In the technological field he was responsible for several apparent advances. The failure to derive benefit from sailing trials, and the need for a more impartial institutionalised system of considering proposals for improvements in steam as well as sailing ships, led him to propose the 'committee of reference'. Under Cockburn, the use of steam in the fleet not only grew but became more acceptable with the rapid introduction of the screw propeller, his aspirations for which were certainly ahead of actual developments. In the evolution of the officer corps and in the management of seamen he was successful only in holding the ground: in emphasising that professional consider-ations should take priority over political ones in appointments; and in resisting those who wish to abolish impressment and summary punish-ment. In this last respect, some would certainly have viewed Cockburn's views as retrograde. Yet he himself would not; indeed, he would have claimed a relative advance, for to have given ground would in his view have been detrimental to the Navy. It was a view that becomes more understandable with an appreciation of the absence of any alternative to impressment, which in turn reveals the importance of Cockburn's contribution to the development of a register of qualified masters and mates in the merchant service through the introduction of voluntary examinations of competence.

This contribution to the development in the long-term of an effective naval reserve perhaps most typified Cockburn's whole contribution to the evolution of the Navy: low-key, depending on administrative insight, organisation, and evolving naturally from contemporary naval thought and circumstances. It was a contribution that people like Briggs as a young man and other civilians cannot have immediately appreciated. For it depended on a confident understanding of the Navy and how it operated far deeper than they as civilians could have possessed. But it was wisdom that people of a similar political complexion like Peel and Haddington appreciated, and for which Cockburn even now should be better respected. Cockburn may have *appeared* the archetypal reactionary, but he was not fundamentally opposed to progress and without doubt, in spite of numerous administrative difficulties, he made his own contribution to the evolution of the Navy at a time of noticeably quickening change.

NOTES

1. C.J. Bartlett, *Great Britain and Sea Power 1815–1853* (Oxford, 1963), appendix III, 342.
2. Bartlett, 7.
3. Sir J. Briggs, *Naval Administrations, 1827–1892* (London, 1897), 11, 75.
4. N[ational] L[ibrary of] S[cotland] MS 2287, f.205, Cockburn to Sir Thomas Cochrane, 26 July 1846.
5. B[ritish] L[ibrary], Add.MS, 40,458, f.271, Lord Haddington to Sir Robert Peel.
6. Selections from the Phinn Committee of Inquiry of October–November 1855 into the state of the Office of Secretary to the Admiralty', appendix 1, ed. C.I. Hamilton, in *The Naval Miscellany*, vol.5, (N[avy] R[ecords] S[ociety], vol. 125, London, 1984), 431–2.
7. *Opinions of the late Right Honourable Sir George Cockburn Bt. G.C.B., Admiral of the Fleet, on the necessity of remodelling the Admiralty Board* (London, 1855), 4–5.
8. S[cottish] R[ecord] O[ffice], GD51/2/739, Haddington to Lord Melville, 26 March 1842. 'Buntade' was presumably derived from the verb 'to bunt' meaning *inter alia* to block a ball.
9. *Opinions*, 5–6.
10. 'Selections ...' (NRS, vol. 125), 391; *Minutes of evidence taken before the Select Committee on the Board of Admiralty*, B[ritish] P[arliamentary] P[apers] 1861 (438), 280, 284.

140

11. Sir Charles Middleton in the 1780s complained of commissioners who 'came and went as inclination had them ... and when they pleased to meddle, ... [had] all the importance of office'. R.A. Morriss, *The Royal Dockyards during the Revolutionary and Napoleonic wars* (Leicester, 1983), 150.
12. *Opinions*, 6.
13. Briggs, 73.
14. P[ublic] R[ecord] O[ffice], ADM 3/265, n.d. [c. April 1843].
15. Bartlett, 222; N.A.M. Rodger, *The Admiralty* (Lavenham, 1979), 101.
16. PRO, ADM 3/265, 'Naval Officers in Coast Guard Services', n.d. [c. April 1842].
17. Briggs, 67.
18. See, for example, his proposal for a change in captain's pay, in PRO, ADM. 3/265, n.d. [c. April 1843].
19. *Opinions*, 7.
20. Briggs, 67, 74.
21. *Opinions*, 7.
22. Windsor, Royal Archives, M51/100, Haddington to Prince Albert, 20 Jan. 1843.
23. NLS, MS 2284, ff. 99, 130; 2285, f. 27; 2286, f. 213, Cockburn to Sir T. Cochrane, 5 Aug., 6 Dec. 1843, 6 Feb. 1844, 7 July 1845; N[ational] M[aritime] M[useum], PLL/6a, Cockburn to Sir W. Pell, I Nov. 1844.
24. Bartlett, 148, 152–4, appendix I, 339–40.
25. Bartlett, 152–3, appendix II, 341.
26. Briggs, 71.
27. PRO, ADM 3/265, n.d. [c. Apr.1843].
28. Bartlett, 158, 170, appendix III, 342.
29. PRO, ADM 3/265, n.d. [c. Apr. 1843].
30. Briggs, 12.
31. G. Penn, *Up Funnel, Down Screw! the story of the naval engineer* (London, 1955), 22.
32. W.L. Clements Library, University of Michigan, Croker papers, Cockburn to J.W. Croker, 12 Sep. 1830.
33. Bartlett, 342.
34. Speeches in the House of Commons, 1 Mar. 1844, 31 Mar. 1845 in *Hansard*, LXXIII, 481; LXXVIII, 1261, 1265.
35. Speech, 4 Mar. 1842, *Hansard*, LXI, 99.
36. Speech, 13 Feb. 1845, *Hansard*, LXXVII, 412.
37. NMM, Croker papers, CKE/6, J.W. Croker to Cockburn, 26 Feb. 1845.
38. BL, Add.MS 40,458, f. 241, Cockburn to Haddington, 15 Nov. 1845. The proposal appears to have been submitted to the rest of the board, for which see PRO, ADM 3/265, n.d..
39. BL, Add.MS 40,458, ff. 246, 259, 266–7, Haddington to Peel, 26 Dec. 1845, Peel to Haddington, 27 Dec. 1845, and Ellenborough's comments, n.d.; J. Fincham, *A History of Naval Architecture* (London, 1851; reprint 1979), 334.
40. Speech, 17 June 1846, *Hansard*, LXXXVII, 627.
41. Speech, 23 May 1845, *Hansard*, LXXX, 816.
42. BL, Add. MS 40,515, f.325, Cockburn to Peel, 23 Sep. 1842; Fincham, 333.
43. Fincham, 333–4, 401, 403.

44. Fincham, 333–4.
45. Speech, 23 May 1845, *Hansard*, LXXX, 820.
46. For details of the French vessels, see S.S. Roberts, 'The French transatlantic steam packet programme of 1840', *Mariner's Mirror*, 73 (1987), 273–86.
47. BL, Add.MS 40,458, f. 57, 'Memo for Lord Haddington in consequence of the note of Sir Charles Napier to Sir Robert Peel', 9 Jun. 1845.
48. BL, Add.MS 40,572, f. 250, Cockburn to Peel, 16 Aug. 1845.
49. G.S. Graham, 'The transition from paddle-wheel to screw propeller', *Mariner's Mirror*, XLIV (1958), 35–48; D.K. Brown, 'The introduction of the screw propeller into the Royal Navy', *Warship* I (1977), 59–63; A. Lambert, 'The Navy and the introduction of the screw propeller, 1837–47', in S. Fisher, ed., *Innovation in Shipping and Trade* (Exeter Maritime Studies, No. 6, Exeter, 1989), 61–88.
50. Dr Lambert's work is particularly valuable in placing these developments in sequence and I am grateful to him for a number of references.
51. PRO, ADM 1/614, minute of 21 Jan. 1842.
52. Speeches, *Hansard*, LXXIII, 472; LXXX, 816.
53. BL, Add.MS 40,458, f. 57,'Memo for Lord Haddington...', 9 June 1845.
54. Graham, 44; Brown, 62.
55. J.H. Baxter, *The Introduction of the Ironclad Warship* (Cambridge, Mass., 1933), 35–6; Bartlett, 218; Fincham, 391. The latter lists 28 iron steamers ordered between 1841 and 1846, 13 propelled by paddles, 15 by screw.
56. Baxter, 37–9.
57. Speeches, 4 Mar. 1842, *Hansard*, LXI, 92, 106; see also Cockburn's evidence, 30 Aug. 1852, before the Committee on Manning, in 'Naval Papers', BPP 1859 (45), and in NMM, PHL/5/1.
58. These demands did in fact result in a decline in the number of men physically punished from 1 in every 17 men in 1839 to 1 in 33 men by 1846: see Bartlett, 312, fn. 2.
59. Washington D.C., Library of Congress, Cockburn papers, letters sent, private, container 13, Cockburn to Lord Aukland, 10 Aug. 1835.
60. Speech, 16 May 1845, *Hansard*, LXXX, 447.
61. BL, Add.MS 40,458, ff. 77, 92, 110, Haddington to Peel, 18 Jun. 1845, and Peel to Haddington, 2 Jul. 1845; see also Cockburn's evidence before the Committee on Manning; Bartlett, 306–7.
62. PRO, ADM 7/714, 'Proposal for establishing a naval reserve', 23 Dec. 1844.
63. Lib. of Congress, Cockburn papers, Letters sent, miscellany, cont. 12, Cockburn to W.S. Gladstone, 9 Feb., 21 Dec. 1844.
64. N. Cox, 'The records of the Registrar General of Shipping and Seamen', *Maritime History*, 2 (1972), 168–88; F.C. Bowen, *History of the Royal Navy Reserve* (London, 1926), 11–20.
65. BL, Add.MS 40,550, ff. 117, 119, Peel to Cockburn, Cockburn to Peel, both 17 Aug. 1844.
66. Ibid, ff. 119, Cockburn to Peel, 17 Aug. 1844, ; M. Lewis, *The Navy in Transition* (London, 1965), 149.
67. Lewis, 116–121; BL, Add.MS 40,458, ff. 283–304, Haddington to Peel, 12–18 Jan. 1846.
68. *Opinions*, 11, 16.

69. PRO, ADM 3/265, n.d. [c. Nov. 1841].
70. NLS, MS 2283, f. 102, Cockburn to Sir T. Cochrane, 4 May 1842.
71. Lib. of Congress, Cockburn papers, letters sent, miscellany, cont. 12, Cockburn to Lady Nicholson, 3 Mar. 1846.
72. See N. Rodger, *The Wooden World. An Anatomy of the Georgian Navy* (London, 1986), 341; D. Bonner Smith, ed., *The Letters of Lord St Vincent*, II (NRS, vol. 61, 1927), 167, 176–7.
73. Lib. of Congress, Cockburn papers, letters sent, miscellany, cont. 12, Cockburn to Sir T. Cochrane, 6 Dec. 1844.

Notes on Contributors

David Davies is Head of History at Bedford Modern School and author of *Gentlemen and Tarpaulins: The Officers and Men of the Restoration Navy* (Oxford, 1991).

Jeremy Black is Reader in History at the University of Durham, author of many books and articles on British foreign policy and the impact upon it of the navy, and co-editor with Philip Woodfine of *The British Navy and the Use of Naval Power in the Eighteenth Century* (Leicester, 1988).

Michael Duffy is a Senior Lecturer in History and Co-Director of the Centre for Maritime Historical Studies at the University of Exeter. His publications include *Soldiers, Sugar and Seapower. The British Expeditions to the West Indies and the War against Revolutionary France* (Oxford, 1987) and he is currently Editor of *The Mariner's Mirror. The Journal of the Society for Nautical Research*.

Nicholas Rodger is an Honorary Research Fellow of the Centre for Maritime Historical Studies at Exeter, and Anderson Research Fellow at the National Maritime Museum, Greenwich. His many publications on the Royal Navy include *The Admiralty* (Lavenham, 1979) and *The Wooden World. An Anatomy of the Georgian Navy* (London, 1986). He is currently writing a multi-volume history of the Royal Navy.

Roger Morriss is Keeper of Manuscripts at the National Maritime Museum, Greenwich. His publications include *The Royal Dockyards during the Revolutionary and Napoleonic Wars* (Leicester, 1983).